# THE
# PURGE

FRANK SCHNEIGER

# THE PURGE

"All arrogance will reap a harvest rich in tears. God calls men to a heavy reckoning for overweening pride."
Herodotus

"...According to what I know of history, I see that mankind could never do without scapegoats."
Gletkin, the jailer in *Darkness at Noon*

"History is made by people who do not know what is going to happen next."
Lawrence Freedmen, *The Future of War*

"The art of prophesy is very difficult, especially with respect to the future."
Mark Twain

"We should always beware that what now lies in the past once lay in the future."
T.W. Maitland

\* \* \*

"The land flourished because it was fed from so many sources — because it was nourished by so many cultures and traditions and people."
President Lyndon Johnson.

"You can call it mysticism if you want to, but I have always believed that there was some divine plan that placed this great continent between two oceans to be sought out by those who were possessed of an abiding love of freedom and a special kind of courage."
President Ronald Reagan

"Democracy does require a basic sense of solidarity — the idea that for all our outward differences, we are all in this together; that we rise or fall as one."
President Barack Obama

FRANK SCHNEIGER

"The concept of global warming was created by and for the Chinese in order to make U.S. manufacturing non-competitive.                    Donald Trump

"Sorry losers and haters, but my I.Q. is one of the highest, and you all know it. Please don't feel so stupid and insecure. It's not your fault."

Donald Trump

"Our country is in serious trouble. We don't have victories anymore. We used to have victories, but we don't have them. I beat China all the time. All the time.

Donald Trump

"Nobody knows the system better than me, which is why I alone can fix it."         Candidate Donald Trump

"I need loyalty. I expect loyalty."

President Donald Trump

"I love to get even. Go for the jugular, attack them in spades....If they screw you, screw them back 10 times as hard. I really believe it."

President Donald Trump

# THE

# PURGE

## THE FUTURE
## AS HISTORY
## IN THE AGE OF
## TRUMP

FRANK SCHNEIGER

NEW YORK

*Dedicated to Bob's Memory*
*and Roberto's Future*


*Special thanks to the Holy Trinity,*
*Irene Jackson, Liz Sheehan and John Devine*

# CONTENTS

# PREAMBLE

*Nineteen-seventeen was a terrible year on earth.* The Great War was in its third horrific year, with industrialized carnage on an unprecedented scale. Within a year, great empires would collapse, vast populations would be displaced, and an inflluenza pandemic would kill between 50- and 100-million people worldwide, compounding the enormous death toll brought on by the war.

Europe would then take a 20-year hiatus before beginning the killing again; this time, the World War would take 40-million lives and produce acts of inhumanity that brought civilization to its lowest point since man began walking upright.

One hundred years later, 2017 was also a terrible year on earth. Vast swaths of the globe were cracking under the combined pressures of overpopulation, misrule and environmental disaster. Syria and Yemen were in the final stages of destruction from prolonged civil war. The post-war structures that had produced a long period of peace, growth and stability were crumbling. And the culture of doubt created by the fossil-fuel industry and its allies was finally giving way to the reality that the future had arrived in the form of heat, fires, floods, and extreme weather events, producing human dislocation and tragedy.

In the United States, the world's most powerful country, the future also arrived in 2017. A half-century of reactionary politics, spawned by "white backlash," corporate power and an obsession with wealth at any price, had culminated in the insertion into the presidency of a mentally ill, cognitively impaired, narcissistic criminal. Behaviors, policies and appointments to high office that would have been unthinkable just a year earlier were now normal. Out-and-out fascists occupied positions of power in the White House and in federal agencies. Moderate Americans began to place their hope in conservative generals, as fear of the sociopath at the top made devotion to the notion of civilian control of the military a fading memory.

Through the early months of the administration, months dominated by a constant stream of "breaking news," almost all produced by the president's actions and statements, there was little comment on the reality that the country was now being run for the benefit of the president and his family along with a handful of ultra-rich plutocrats and corporations. Meanwhile, the administration's base of support, virtually all white and including racists, fascists and neo-Nazis, was placated with ongoing attacks on the "others": immigrants, minorities, and the hated "liberals." Along with, as the downward spiral accelerated, the eternal scapegoat: "the Jews."

All of this was obscured by pervasive confidence in American exceptionalism, the belief that, even though the United States looked more like Argentina or Vichy France, everything in the end would work out, because it always did, right? The Shining City on the Hill. And we would still be Number One.

For decades, Republicans and their allies had used the phrase "the American people" to define a specific group: white, conservative, well-off, suburban Christians. And these real Americans would always come out all right. As for the others, things may not turn out so well. But they had been so "otherized" that many people weren't that concerned. And, in the future, these white Americans could always contend that they didn't know what terrible things had been done in their name.

America, the land of denial and self-deception, was also the land of prediction. And, for the religious predictors, the land of prophesy. There was a lot of prophesy. Mark Twain once said, "Prophesy is a good line of business, but it is full of risks." Far earlier, and more to the point, Lao Tzu remarked, "Those who have knowledge, don't predict. Those who predict don't have knowledge." The United States had become a nation of knowledge-free predictors.

The narratives that follow are not a prediction of future events. The range of potential unexpecteds is extensive, and, as that philosopher of our times Roseanne Roseannadanna repeatedly reminded us,

"It's always something." These narratives describe one possible set of outcomes. They are outcomes that most would consider implausible, but as our institutions buckle, our deep divisions seem increasingly unbridgeable, and the moral bankruptcy of our elites becomes inescapable, these outcomes — through a process of elimination — become more likely.

These narratives are thematic and essentially chronological, but their order and content also reflect the speed at which events overtake reality on an almost daily basis in our times. By the time you read this, the ground may have shifted in ways that were unimaginable just months ago.

The line from unimaginable to unlikely to possible and then inevitable is often much shorter than we think.

# PART ONE
## THE RUN-UP

## THE OPTIONS:
### *This Can't Go On*

*Although most people avoided discussing them,* the options became quite clear at a surprisingly early date. In the end, there were only five potential outcomes. It could go on for four, or possibly even eight, years. It was never clear how many people believed that this was possible, and many understood that the country would be unrecognizable and riven with hatred, violence and even more extreme inequality if that happened.

In the film *The Gatekeepers*, in describing how Israel had changed as a result of the occupation of the West Bank, a former head of the Israeli security services says, "We have become a cruel nation." The United States had become a cruel nation, in the sense that a cruel but large minority was now in control.

It could end in the president's resignation, probably in a deal for a pardon for his, his family's, and his associates' criminal offenses. These pardons would cover the president and his immediate family members. Others would not be so lucky. The scale of criminality and the number of those involved made this option problematic, and, as time went on, increasingly unlikely.

The 25th Amendment could be invoked, as it became inescapable that the president was mentally incompetent and cognitively impaired. That would require action by cabinet members and congressional leaders who were complicit in a broad range of misdeeds and who knew of the president's mental illness from well before his inauguration. Another unlikely outcome.

It could end in impeachment, which, given Republican fecklessness and moral bankruptcy, along with the Party's growing dependence on extremist elements for election, seemed quite improbable.

Or, finally, it could end in the unthinkable: a military takeover of the government when the civilian branches proved incapable of doing their duty. Few thought of this possibility. We were exceptional. Coups were the kind of thing that happened in Argentina or Nigeria.

## ROT AND CORRUPTION:
### *They All Knew*
---

For many months, people had said, "This can't go on." But it did. The fact that the president was mentally ill and showing increasing signs of dementia became undeniable despite some skillful handling that allowed him to sound rational during his few televised addresses to the nation. His appointments and policies fit classic definitions of fascism. That the undermining and destruction of the federal government was a strategy rather than an unintended outcome was clear to anyone with eyes. We can't go on like this. But we did.

Even more damning was the toxic spread of corruption, and the unmistakable sense that the United States had become just another kleptocracy, a Brazil or the Philippines. The self-enrichment of family members, hangers-on, criminals and collaborators became so blatant that all but hard-core true believers were appalled. The realization that wealthy members of Congress had voted themselves huge tax cuts, and then lied about it, barely caused a ripple. Why should that surprise anyone?

What continued to surprise observers was the steadfastness of those true believers. These were people who remained supportive as long as two conditions were met: the search for scapegoats continued, and their media avatars fed them lies that they wanted to believe. They defined their world by their hatreds, and they had come to believe in and to identify a new hated enemy: The Deep State.

This can't go on like this. But it did. Congress, under firm Republican control, proved itself to be more morally bankrupt than even the most cynical had thought possible. The administration's efforts to discredit a free press were largely successful, producing a country so deeply polarized by hatred that even those who believed in American exceptionalism were terrified. When the president attacked the law enforcement agencies investigating his crimes, Republicans in Congress either joined the attack or remained silent.

But the right-wing, white, "Christian" base held together. As one observer noted, they were the group that espoused a clear set of peculiarly American Christian values: hatred of Obama and Clinton; hatred of liberals; hatred of the others, (gay people, minorities and immigrants); hatred of the media, and hatred of abortion. Check the boxes and, despite everything else, their support would remain solid.

In a very short time, roundups, mass deportations and the destruction of families had become normalized. The system of secret, private, for-profit prisons expanded; human rights violations became the norm, and the existence of fascist and racist pockets in the immigration and border patrol services became impossible to cover up. Voices of protest were stifled. Men with shaved heads, sunglasses and earpieces seemed to be everywhere. It couldn't go on like this. But it did.

As repression increased and individual freedoms withered, America's corporate and other elites remained largely silent, comfortable with the first truly business-friendly administration in years. Only when the president did something so outrageous that it couldn't be allowed to pass were carefully calibrated, largely sanitized statements of criticism issued.

And, as for "the masses," their responses once again reinforced the accuracy of Tolstoy's quote in *Anna Karenina*: "There are no conditions to which a person cannot become accustomed, especially if they see everyone around them living in the same way." Life went on, especially if you minded your own business, and you didn't have the misfortune of being a member of a scapegoat group.

A large group of Americans, the president's support base, could not be criticized. Part of the right-wing mantra was that these groups had been disrespected, ignored and considered stupid and ignorant by the liberal elites. (That many of them were, in fact, stupid, ignorant and bigoted could not be openly stated.) So they were often treated with a respect and deference that they hardly deserved.

As a result, many of the president's fans missed something fundamental: A deep loathing of the President's all-white base was growing in many segments of the population, a loathing that would have shocked them, so totally had they convinced themselves of their own victimhood and innocence.

Senior military officers in an administration full of generals may have been troubled by some of it, but like the corporate and financial elites, they were getting everything they asked for, both institutionally and personally. In the world of pervasive temptation that the president, his family and top aides had created, most of the generals, just like almost everyone else with access to the honey pot, succumbed

Through it all, even as the president and his administration reneged on — or lied about — every promise they had made to their base, his approval ratings never dipped below 30 percent. His fans, the addicted viewers and listeners to Nation's News and far-right talk radio, believed all the lies, and increasingly attributed the president's failures to The Deep State, the government traitors who were seeking to undermine him.

The Deep State became an article of faith and a justification for ongoing repression. In a society already marked by deep levels of mistrust, those levels were now blended with actively cultivated suspicion and hatred to produce a toxic stew that was used to justify the most extreme actions. As a liberal commentator said, "We're all Muslims now."

To the extent that he governed at all, the president governed as if his increasingly narrow constituency were "the American people." And to keep them at bay, he and his team understood that if they couldn't deliver any improvement in their lives, which they obviously could not, they had to intensify the search for scapegoats and enemies.

The administration became a one-trick pony, and that trick was otherization, stirring the hatred of minorities, poor people, immigrants, Muslims and, most of all, liberals and the so-called liberal media, which became the most hated groups and the most visible targets of far-right violence and intimidation.

The president's tacky Nuremberg-style rallies now took on far more menacing qualities. Unable to accurately claim any positive achievements, tax cuts for the rich being a tough sell, the focus on scapegoats and the glorification of violence became the sole focus. There was no more talk of jobs for coal miners or "great" health care. In place of "Lock her up!" chants aimed at his former opponent, with the previously flourishing economy slowing, the nation increasingly isolated in the world, and the health-care system in a downward spiral, the president and his tiny group of key aides now responded favorably to audience cries for exterminating liberals and, the historic favorite, the deportation of Jews.

No longer did the president fend off the charges of anti-Semitism by pointing to his Jewish family members. His advisers had told him that calling attention to having Jews in his family was hurting him with the base. He got the message.

Liberal media outlets were threatened and, in several instances, fire bombed. In the incident that got the most attention, the host of a liberal cable-news show was poisoned and forced off the air for months. By the time it happened, it all seemed normal, and, in now standard operating procedure, Nation's News and the president's faithful web and radio outlets hinted that the poisoning was a hoax or a "false-flag" attack.

In one of its many 5-4 decisions, the Supreme Court upheld a recently passed law that made it a crime of treason to publish leaked "secret" documents. Just so no one missed the point, the opinion was written by the Court's newest member, the president's appointee, who, in his confirmation hearing, had repeated the worn-out mantra that he would just "call balls and strikes."

## THE GREAT DIVIDE

During this period, two contradictory ideas were held in equilibrium at the highest levels of society. One was a sense that this could not go on forever, and the other a feeling of impunity on the part of both new and established elites. Whatever happened, and whatever they had done or whomever they had collaborated with, they would be invulnerable. And in both respects, history, especially American history, with some infrequent exceptions, was on their side. They chose to ignore those exceptions.

It was interesting that phrases associated with French corruption and decay began to pop up to describe America's situation, phrases like *enrichessez vous, sauve qui peut* and *fin de siecle*. "Grab what you can because this isn't going to go on forever." It seemed clever at the time, but there was another French word that would turn out to have shocking relevance in the immediate future. That word was *epuration*, purification, or more precisely, "purge."

As the administration tore itself apart internally, mostly over money and fears of criminal indictment, it sought to present a different picture to the outside world. That was the picture of the smart businessmen and generals doing the people's work, cleaning up the terrible mess that had been left to them and restoring the nation's greatness.

The enormous chasm dividing Americans widened as people increasingly lived in two information worlds, one based largely on fact and the other shaped by lies. But they were lies that the president's fans wanted to believe because they justified their bigotry, their grasping, and their sense of victimization and entitlement. Believing them also paved the way for the justification *We just didn't know*, in case things didn't go their way.

For those religiously watching Nation's News, consulting neo-fascist web sites or listening to far-right radio, the destruction of democracy and the wave of corruption were not the stories. The stories were the crimes — especially sex crimes — committed by illegal immigrants; the efforts of the Deep State to undermine the president; the transgressions of the previous administration, and the lies being told by the "media".

And in almost every case, the victims were white, the perpetrators people of color and foreigners, and the defenders of the perpetrators were invariably the hated liberals. When the administration's crime was so egregious and obvious that it couldn't be disputed, the response was always the same: The Democrats are even worse.

Those in the administration believed that they could run the country on behalf of their plutocrat allies and retain the support of the all-white 30-percent minority, which included racist and fascist elements that the Republican Party now depended on for election. Nazis were no longer "outside the tent." In fact, the president had referred to them as fine people.

The daily diet of outrageous statements and actions by the president obscured the revolution in government and American life that was taking place. Congress had passed tax cuts ordered up by the corporations and rich donors who now ran the country. They then proceeded to go on a spending binge, justified, as always, as being essential to support "the troops."

These tax cuts and the content of the legislation made clear that the gulf between the nation's plutocratic and corporate elites and ordinary Americans was so vast that it could not be bridged. The administration reflected the greed of the richest Americans, people for whom there would never be enough, and of the corporate leaders whose only goals were shareholder value and personal enrichment.

While they had contempt for the president and his team of arrivistes, fascists and parasites, corporate America was getting everything it wanted. And its arrogance and insularity from American life cultivated a sense of impunity and imperviousness. They could not imagine any consequence for themselves. After all, just a decade earlier this same group had wrecked the economy, impoverished millions and walked away with a few slaps on the wrist. And now, even those slaps on the wrist seemed impossible to imagine.

Within the federal government, revolutionary changes were taking place at a rate that no one could keep up with. The State Department had been devastated by an arch-criminal who had covered up the realities of climate change for decades, and virtually every other department, except the Department of Defense, was being criminalized and turned over to corporate interests. Fifty percent of the defense budget now went to contractors, as opposed to "the troops."

Through it all, the 30 percent remained steadfast, their sense of white victimization, their ignorance of either history or current reality, and their willingness to countenance the vast cruelty of their government, had all been either justified or masked by the process of otherization that the Republican Party had built its success on for decades.

And, on a daily basis, the president and his helpers fed them the red meat that would keep them on board, while Nation's News and the other increasingly fascist and semi-official news outlets lied to them about what was happening. Much of America missed this; when asked if they ever watched Nation's News, they would laugh and say no, that they couldn't stand it. But the 30 percent *could* stand it. In fact, they were addicted to it.

## THE GREAT MISCONCEPTION

All these groups, from the elites to the "little people," operated under one big misconception, a misconception that would permanently upset the national apple cart. It was the belief that, in an increasingly militarized society, the military was cohesive and driven by universally shared values. And that if those who had never served just continued to heap praise on the troops and "our great vets, we love our vets," the military would always go along with the program.

And, finally, the crowning misconception: the belief by those now in power, politically and financially, that whatever they did, the military would always be on their side.

They were wrong.

To a group of younger senior officers, there was a growing sense that American society was in a downward spiral, that their superior officers had made a bargain with the devil by becoming part of a fascist administration, and that the administration — including its generals — posed a grave danger to the country, the world and, most immediately, to the soldiers, sailors and marines under their command.

For the most part, these officers, overwhelmingly conservative Christians, could not abide the moral decay, corruption and powerful hatreds that had now spread to the military itself, a force that had over recent decades increasingly — and dangerously — seen itself as being morally superior to the society that it ostensibly served.

These officers had been strongly influenced by the thinking of a senior commander who was now teaching at an Ivy League university. He had retired and become a major critic of the militarization of American society and its foreign policy. He had a strong following among this band of younger senior officers, who saw their leadership responsibility in moral terms.

This group had watched developments, first with a sense of unease, then concern and finally alarm, as what passed for policy came out of the White House and was implemented by men and women that they had respected over the years. They were coming to view their former mentors and role models as collaborators in something fundamentally wrong. They sensed that the president and his top aides loved violence as an end in itself. The word evil crept into the conversations of serious men and women when they discussed what was occurring. There were long discussions about what constituted a lawful order.

There did not appear to be a single tipping point that pushed this group of officers over the edge; nor was it a single ambitious leader who spurred them to action. Instead, there was something organic and cumulative about the events that would upend American society and reverse trends that had been many decades in the making.

It was not a case of *drip, drip, drip* that pushed them, because the driving events and actions were of such a magnitude that they went far beyond being drips. It was their sheer volume that made them seem like drips, particularly as they related to the destruction of the institutions on which American democracy rested.

The first seminal event was the opening of largely secret prisons for immigrants, along with those found guilty of sedition or similar political crimes. These prisons were owned and managed by private for-profit companies, linked to a cabinet member. However, to improve the bottom line, the Marine Corps was ordered to provide security.

Then there was the revival of torture and the use of the infamous black sites, blots on America's record that could not be erased, and which the president seemed to view as an end rather than what he referred to as a tool. The goal was inflicting pain, not securing information. And there were many like thinkers in Congress. During the State of the Union address, Republicans thought it was worth of a standing ovation when the president promised to keep the Guantanamo Bay prison open.

Next was the relaxation of rules of engagement, and the rumor that senior officials, apparently including the president, viewed collateral damage not as an unfortunate side effect, but as a good thing in and of itself: a pre-emptive reduction in the potential terrorist population. These officers were stunned to find that extremist members of Congress, leaders of hate groups and the president's family members were regularly included in White House military policy discussions, and that their comments were often overtly racist.

What was never discussed by the president and his team was the effect of their decisions on those required to carry them out. They never thought much about those who would do the torturing, or those responsible for the multiple deaths of women and children. The officers began to realize that, like those on the receiving end, these soldiers were also just an abstraction, and that all the glorification of the troops and "our great vets" was just part of the package of lies.

While leaks had been dramatically reduced by the draconian punishments imposed on those who had been caught, reports about the president's demand for details about methods of torture and what was happening at the black sites continued to seep out. All denied or obfuscated by his press spokespersons.

"This can't go on like this." But it did. And, as it did, the unthinkable became more thinkable.

## ANOTHER RED FLAG:
### *"The Government Army"*

In their efforts to undermine public education and pave the way for privatization of schools at every level, the reactionary right had begun to refer to public schools as "government" schools. For that portion of the public that had been primed for the past four decades to hate government, it was a clever move.

And it worked in generating hostility in other areas as well, so that "government lands" and "government programs" became rallying points for privatization that someone or some private equity group saw as a moneymaking opportunity. In this way, a society that had a market economy had become a market society, and government a constant target of disdain.

Josh Williams was a Brigadier General in the United States Army and a West Point graduate. His best friend Ray Guzman was a marine and also a Brigadier General, assigned to the Secretary of Defense. Early on a rainy July morning, Williams called Guzman. They had the following conversation:

"Ray, did you see this?"

(Pause) "Okay, what is *this?*"

"Don't give me that; you know exactly what *thi*s is."

"Oh, yes, I believe that I am aware of the matter to which you are referring."

"Right. Did the Secretary go along with this?"

"Worse than you think."

"What?"

"He didn't know about it."

"What do you mean?"

"I've got to go."

The "this" that the two were obliquely discussing was a proposed plan to privatize the ongoing war in Afghanistan, now the longest war in American history. The founder of a mercenary army who had become a major contractor in America's other wars was now proposing to replace the United States military in Afghanistan, a military that was now being referred to — in mildly disparaging tones — as the "government army." The contractor and his mercenaries would do it way more cheaply and would not be bound by the kinds of rules of engagement that prevent torture and summary execution of prisoners.

By all accounts, the president liked the idea a lot, as did family members and others in the inner circle, especially those who had been secretly promised enormous kickbacks.

For Williams and Guzman, along with others, this news went far beyond being insulting: It represented a threat to the Republic. They were shocked that it had even gotten a hearing, let alone being seriously considered by leaders who had already revealed a vast ignorance of the military. And that senior military leaders had been cut out of the conversation.

A seed had been planted. That seed would grow and have enormous consequences. When the two generals got together for dinner and a movie later that week, the film that they watched was *Seven Days in May*.

## CLIMATE CHANGE:
### *The Unexpected Catalyst*

The environment and climate change are generally not considered to be preoccupations of the military, but in the United States they had been for decades. The Department of Defense had invested significant time and money and created a specialized unit in seeking to understand climate change's security implications.

The DOD had come to an obvious conclusion: Climate change posed a grave threat to world stability, and by extension to America's national security. For example, it found a clear link between climate change and Syria's descent into its catastrophic civil war. Knowing they would be ridiculed and accused of overreach, the Department kept these findings under wraps.

Their analyses also projected that major coastal defense facilities, such as the base at Newport News, would be underwater in the decades ahead if action wasn't taken, and that trillions of dollars of infrastructure would be destroyed. And the threat was not just in the future: Homestead Air Base, in Florida, and Keesler Air Force Base, in Mississippi, had been destroyed by hurricanes Andrew and Katrina. It had cost well in excess of one billion dollars to rebuild them.

The officer in charge of this unit watched the president's speech withdrawing the United States from the Paris Climate Accords. He had successfully educated Secretaries of Defense on this issue for the past 15 years. None had been more receptive than the current Secretary, who had read voraciously on the subject but now remained mute as the President of the United States presented a litany of lies and distortions to justify his actions. A guidance had come from the White House: Mind your own business.

In addition to the lies and distortions, the officer noticed two other things that frightened him. The first was the cult of personality that was being created around the president. The sycophancy of the vice president and cabinet members, and praise of the president's "leadership" was so effusive that it crossed several lines and fed into the "only I...." narrative that the president had spun during his campaign. Government events took on the air of an all-white North Korean Communist Party Congress, which along with the Nuremberg-style rallies were increasingly difficult to reconcile with democracy, as was the president's assertion that those who didn't clap for him were committing treason.

Ignorant and flippant climate-change-denial remarks were a regular staple in these events.

The second profoundly disturbing attribute of the president's climate-change speech was his constant references to American victimization and the false notion that, at least until now, the United States had been the laughing stock of the world. The president was nurturing a nation of victims.

The officer was a cautious man. The evening after the climate-change-withdrawal speech, he struggled first to fully understand what was happening, and then, more importantly, to figure out what he had to do. He surfed the cable news channels and stopped to watch a group discussion on Nation's News. One of the commentators, who cultivated the image of a wise punk, accused his fellow panelists of not having read the studies, which he said he had and which, he asserted, debunked climate science. He finished by pointing out that he had gone to a top university, a strange badge of honor on a channel that prided itself on speaking to the great unwashed and that demeaned knowledge and learning.

For some reason, it was this cable news discussion and not the president's speech that was the straw that broke the camel's back. He placed a call to a home at Fort McNair. This was the conversation. "It's late." "I know. I'll be there." "Good. You know, sometimes just understanding isn't enough." "I know. Goodnight."

The team was coming together. And it would include the right people.

## THE INFLECTION POINT

If there was a last straw for the group, it was a meeting with the president, the national security staff and the president's political advisors and family members. The subject was North Korea and the response to its provocations. The part of the discussion that leaked out and got back to the group of officers was the near total indifference to the fact that 20 million South Koreans living in Seoul might be killed by North Korean artillery as a result of American military action.

One of the president's closest advisors was reported to have done a takeoff on the film *Dr. Strangelove*, with the riff, "I'm not saying that we wouldn't get our hair mussed." Except that the "we" he was talking about consisted almost entirely of Koreans. One of the president's children was reported to have said, in referring to the 20 million South Koreans, "Hey, sometimes you have to take one for the team." These comments reportedly evoked laughter from the president and the assembled group.

There were consistent reports that this combination of ignorance, shallowness, recklessness and cruelty was the subtext of almost every meeting with the president. A second theme was the president's lack of interest in or knowledge of anything in the world that did not touch on one of his investments. He did not know where countries were on the map, who the members of NATO were or any of the critical history of world events.

A White House aide described the president to one of the officers as a "malignant version of Chauncey Gardiner," the television-watching idiot in the film *Being There*. A tell-all book appeared in which virtually the entire White House staff was reported to consider the president an incompetent. Terms like "moron," "crazy," "stupid," and "asshole" were regularly used to describe him by people in high positions.

All these officers had worked with egomaniacs; it was an occupational hazard. But this was different: A cult of personality was being nurtured around a man who cared nothing for his country, was woefully ignorant, and whose motivating forces consisted entirely of greed, celebrity attention, racial bigotry and revenge.

The officers came to a fundamental conclusion: This cannot go on, and we have to stop it.

Quite abruptly, what had been a kind of study group seeking the right path in treacherous times became a group of conspirators. Their conversations now weighed strategy and tactics against the moral, political and personal consequences of these discussions. Each night they realized they were a step closer to setting in motion actions that would irreversibly change the country they served. And should they fail, if spared the death penalty, would land them in prison for the rest of their lives.

FRANK SCHNEIGER

# PART TWO
## VANISHING OPTIONS –
## THE COUP

### WHY?
#### *The Future in the Rear-view Mirror*

*Why had these discussions taken this turn?*
The group had started with possible justifications. Based
on all available evidence, it easily satisfied itself that
drastic action was not only justified, it was an obligation.
They moved on to consequences and alternatives.

The primary justification was the now irrefutable
but still somewhat hidden reality that the president
was severely mentally ill, and that he was surrounded
by a coterie of advisors who were either fascists, money-
driven financial criminals or part of an insulated, hyper-
arrogant and grasping family-dominated royal court.

Then there was the reality that the brakes that
might have saved the country in the past were either
gone or fatally weakened. The legitimate press, with a
handful of exceptions, was either cowed or controlled
by the same corporate minds that had made peace with
the administration in other sectors. And, in most cases,

the principle of balanced reporting was applied in an environment in which it had little or no relevance.

Congress under Republican control had proven itself from the first days to be morally bankrupt, and those few voices of real opposition were now physically intimidated, either being blackmailed by the administration or on the way out. While everything the President touched was tainted and diminished, no institution would be as sullied as the Congress.

In retrospect, it would be shown that the administration's use of blackmail, in league with its media allies, explained a whole range of behaviors and actions that had previously seemed inexplicable.

The courts occasionally provided token opposition, but they too had been intimidated. Groups of federal judges were reportedly discussing the character of Ernst Janning, in real life Franz Schlegelberger, the esteemed judge in Nazi Germany, who went along with the program and ended up in the dock in the film *Judgment at Nuremberg*. But most of them, socially isolated, part of the ultra-conservative Federalist Society elite, and steeped in American exceptionalism, couldn't make the connection. They soldiered on, reinforcing the corporate state and providing originalist rationales for the rubber-stamping of extremist laws, executive orders and corporate crimes.

Then there was what the officers saw as the corruption of their own revered institution, the military.

There had always been a revolving door between the military and defense contractors, who were now absorbing more than 50 percent of the defense budget, and there had always been "ticket punchers," men and women who saw the military as a necessary stop on their way to getting rich, or first into politics and then getting rich. But these groups were now dominant and coming and going in months rather than years.

And with their comings and goings came a growing indifference to the wellbeing of soldiers, sailors and marines. As always, the person at the top was defining core values and the culture. And, in this culture, there was no place for the little people, even if they wore a uniform.

The president's predecessor, derided as being weak and not sufficiently slavish to the military budget, had spent many long hours visiting wounded soldiers at Washington's military hospitals. His wife led the successful national effort to reduce homelessness among veterans. The current president, however, never visited these soldiers and veterans; nor did any member of his family, none of whom had ever served in the military.

The officers came to some basic conclusions. First, that the president and his inner circle had already done mortal damage to American democracy; second, that these same people posed an incalculable threat to the world and to the American forces that these officers were responsible for; third, that their group was alone, with few if any institutional allies, and, finally, that they could see no imaginable path to improvement.

They decided to overthrow the government of the United States of America.

And as soon as what had been unthinkable became thinkable, it became inevitable. And the inevitable came sooner rather than later.

## ASLEEP AT THE SWITCH

Certain qualities of the administration eased the path to the plotters' success. One was the belief by those in the White House that vast increases in military spending inoculated them from any threat from the armed services. Paranoid about the media, a largely non-existent left and ineffectual liberals, they didn't fear the military. Why should they? They had gotten everything they wanted.

Then there was history. The history of military coups is long and inglorious. It stretches back over the millennia and across all continents, but not North America. Except in the movies, the military had never tried to overthrow an American government. American administrations had sponsored and supported coups around the globe, typically with catastrophic results for the citizens of the unfortunate country, but they had avoided temptation at home.

And even in movies like *Seven Days in May*, the coup threat always came from the far right. As it glorified the military, championed violence, supported white supremacists and neo-Nazis, gutted environmental laws and unraveled what was left of the nation's social safety net, nobody could outflank this administration on the right. They felt safe.

Because of the president's mental disorder, narcissism and incompetence, he surrounded himself with similar people, the small groups that he felt he could trust. They trafficked in rumors and conspiracy theories that they picked up from Nation's News and far-right talk radio hosts. To these groups, the Deep State consisted of liberals, Jews, faceless bureaucrats and their ilk. The enemies were on the left. Not high-ranking military officers, whom the president condescendingly referred to as "my generals."

## THE PATH TO ACTION

The coup was a military operation. And who better to plan a military operation than the best military minds in the country. Secrecy was essential and maintaining it was aided by the fact that those who may have had suspicions about what was going on, things like quickly planned movements and unusual Signal Corps activity, said nothing to anybody. In the back of their minds was the notion that these activities may be the inevitable response to the belief that it can't go on like this.

But maintaining secrecy was made harder by the basic assumption that, given their crimes, large numbers of people, starting with the president but including the complicit and the collaborators (the quislings), could not be allowed to simply walk away with a reprimand. Nor could they be allowed to mount a counter-coup. The circle had to be kept small.

Prisons are closed societies, so once people are incarcerated, it is possible to keep them in total isolation. And there was plenty of prison space in the United States, the world leader in imprisoning people. Here the planners faced four challenges: whom to arrest; where to put them; how to get them there, and then what to do with them. The first three required secrecy. Lists and action orders for roundups were compiled. Those on the lists, all of whom had lived lives defined by impunity and who viewed themselves as invulnerable, would have been shocked to see their names there.

Then the officers took a risky step. Except for the plotting itself, they committed their first illegal act: They secretly transferred all the prisoners being held at Guantanamo Bay to military prisons on the mainland. This was in direct contravention of federal law, but they succeeded. All visits to Guantanamo were suspended because of a "health alert," all communications were banned, and the facilities were given a good cleaning. Those who had either advocated torture or claimed that "Gitmo" was a tropical paradise would be able to experience the property first hand. That was where many of them were going to go.

## THE COUP:
*"The Enemies List"*

Military operations generally don't go smoothly. This one did. The president was arrested at his Florida estate, in bed with one of his female assistants. The Secret Service officers did not "take one for the Chief." They stood aside.

Back in the first days of the administration, the president had appointed the governor of South Carolina as U.S. Ambassador to the United Nations. In her first remarks she said, "You're going to see a change in the way we do business.... For those who don't have our back, we're taking names. We will make points to respond to that accordingly."

It wasn't quite clear what her threat meant, and the ambassador, who apparently got the appointment because the president liked her looks, had become a dependable voice for the administration.

An enterprising columnist took up the concept of making lists and began to publish the names of all those who collaborated with or benefited from some corrupt action on the part of what he referred to as the regime. He said that he hoped his list would someday be the needed antidote to America's "short-term memory problem."

Those on the columnist's ever-growing list had two sets of reactions. For the ones steeped in arrogance, it was a source of amusement, kind of like the liberals who had taken pride in being on Richard Nixon's enemies list. But for others, those with a feel for the impermanence of things, it became a source of concern, and they launched efforts to discredit the columnist and get him fired. It didn't work, and the list became a powerful tool in the hands of the coup planners.

Military people like checklists, and here was a useful one, always up to date and from a reliable source. It would turn out to be the ambassador's good fortune that her marginalization relegated her to the category of Minor Collaborator on the list.

## THE ROUNDUPS

Cabinet members, top aides and the president's court were all taken into custody and sequestered incommunicado at undisclosed locations. The only surprise was that the high-ranking military officers in the administration were not spared the indignity of being arrested. They too were taken to undisclosed locations.

All major media outlets were seized and given a script informing the nation of what had just happened and why. These outlets were provided with a treasure trove of documents that revealed corruption, cynicism, blackmail, racism and incompetence on levels that even the president's legions of haters found shocking.

These documents also made plain that the president's level of mental functioning was so low he could not grasp the simplest concepts, and that those around him, including his own children, constantly played to his biggest needs: constant attention, the desire for revenge and a love of violence.

The president, bewildered and disheveled, demanded to know when he was going back to the White House. He may have understood that his life had taken an irreversible turn for the worse when the soldier nearest him responded, "Never, you motherfucker." The soldier's superior officer did not reprimand him for being disrespectful.

The man who had always taken great satisfaction in denigrating and humiliating others was now getting a taste of his own medicine. And it was just a first taste. The pigeon had become the statue. Many others would soon join him.

FRANK SCHNEIGER

# PART THREE
## THE IMMEDIATE AFTERMATH

### THE FALSE SENSE OF RELIEF:
*Misreading the Uses of History*

*Across the country, there seemed to be a collective* sigh of relief, coupled with a fear of the unknown world that the republic was entering. There had now been a forceful response to "This can't go on".

As the impact of the government's disastrous and corrupt actions and policies had become clear, especially to those who had voted for him in the belief that only the others were going to be screwed, his support had sunk to 30 percent. But that core had never wavered. They held to two views: The charges against the president and the administration were all fake news, and the Democrats are even worse, even though the coup had not been made by Democrats.

This group, the 30 percent, would play a critical role in determining the nation's future.

The president's support had been concentrated in extremist groups that had links to the White House or to friendly members of Congress. It was not as if a popular leader had been deposed. Strangely, in an opinion poll in 2015, Republicans had been more than twice as likely to support a military coup than Democrats. But this had been when the hated Negro was in the Oval Office and loathing of liberals was at fever pitch.

It was surprising that portions of this group of the president's biggest supporters now also seemed to support the military coup that removed him from office. Based on their extremely superficial reading of history, they believed that the military would pursue the same far-right, scapegoat-driven policies as the administration had, but would just do a better job of it, with less embarrassment.

The foolishness of this line of thinking never occurred to most of them. As the French film director Claude Chabrol once said, "Stupidity is infinitely more fascinating than intelligence. Intelligence has its limits, while stupidity has none."

Among those relieved were the Republicans in Congress, much of the media, which now made a pivot to support military dictatorship, and the country's corporate and financial elites, who saw the military as a source of stability for "the markets." The financial and corporate sectors had also already gotten everything they wanted out of the administration in the form of huge tax cuts, regulatory relief and the elimination of any fears of prosecution for corrupt practices. In terms of timing and sequencing, this seemed to be an almost perfect outcome for them.

These beliefs rested on two assumptions: that Americans, as always, would have the world's shortest memories about who did what, and that the culture of impunity for those at the very top, a longstanding norm in American life, would remain in place after the coup. After all, the ones with the money and guns had always been on their side.

This second belief would prove to be their fatal miscalculation. The first hint of that miscalculation came when the now deposed president was brought before a preliminary hearing of a military tribunal. In what seemed like a non-sequitur, one of the first questions asked by the prosecuting officer was, "Have you ever heard of Marshal Petain?"

"Who?"

And the prosecutor began the presentation of the long list of charges against the former president, whose only response was to demand to see his (also incarcerated) sons, daughter, son-in-law and "my Jewish lawyer."

"That will not be possible."

Petain and the post-Vichy French parallels would keep coming, not the least of which was the rush by all kinds of collaborators, sycophants and criminals to audition for their reverse-engineered roles in the Resistance. Members of Congress who were willing to betray their oath of office to cover up the administration's treasonous activities now claimed that they had smelled a rat right from the start and had been trying to get to the bottom of it.

Nation's News, the administration's semi-official state news agency, and its cadre of smart-aleck Joseph Goebbels and big-busted Tokyo Rose talking-head types now became strictly Stars and Stripes television, glorifying the military 24/7 and relegating the president and his inner circle to a Stalinist-like world of non-persons.

The nation's corporate and financial elite, having cashed in, now claimed to be champions of civil liberties and were shocked — shocked! — to find out what had been going on. Public relations departments and consultants were working around the clock to find any piece of evidence that they and their firm, especially its CEO, had been 100 percent anti-fascist from the beginning.

And, of course, nobody knew anybody who had been involved in these criminal activities or, in many cases, had even heard of the president. It was like St. Peter at the foot of the cross when he was asked if he wasn't the friend of Our Lord and Savior: "Jesus? Jesus? No, I don't believe I ever met the man." People who had previously claimed to have the president's ear now asserted that, yes, they may have had a cup of coffee at the White House once, but it was just as part of a tour group.

But in almost all instances, none of these members of the elite were particularly worried about their futures; it had always worked out in the past. The question, "Do you know who I am?" had always served as an insurance policy. And you could always count on the short memories of the American people. But those in charge had the lists, all carefully annotated and documented with descriptions of a range of crimes and misdeeds.

As a result, this time it wouldn't work. Decades of arrogance-driven impunity had numbed their antennae and blinded them to the situation they now faced. They fundamentally misread the nature of the group that had engineered the overthrow. As Herodotus had stated two thousand years earlier, "All arrogance will reap a harvest rich in tears. God calls men to a heavy reckoning for overweening pride." Sometimes man doesn't wait for God and the final reckoning. This would be one of those times.

In the past, the others had reaped the harvest rich in tears: poor people, minorities, working people, immigrants and refugees. The social distance between these otherized groups and the elites was so great that those on top barely acknowledged their existence, let alone their plight. An occasional bone thrown to the increasingly non-existent middle class defined the outer limits of their compassion.

The elites had misjudged the group that had overthrown the government, as well as the moral forces that had driven them. There were two early warning signs, each of which would prove to be of enormous importance. The right-wing had always favored military tribunals over civilian courts. More efficient, more secret, and far more likely to come up with guilty verdicts. Next, these groups were also big fans of capital punishment. Just desserts for these criminals. They were about to change their tune on both matters.

## THE CONSTITUTION AND
## THE SUCCESSION NIGHTMARE

The Constitution had been obliterated in four stages. The first was the wave of criminality that the president and his administration unleashed. The second was the failure of the two other branches of government to deal with the corruption and criminality. The third, precipitated by the first two, was the coup itself. And the fourth was the succession that the Constitution prescribed and the cast of characters in that line of succession.

Contrary to the popular slogan, it wasn't the cover-up that brought down the administration. It was the scale of the crimes that had been committed and the complicity — or at least the acquiescence — of the nation's business and financial elite, the Republican Party and approximately one third of the population.

As soon as the Transition Team considered the Constitution's order of succession, it became clear that it was a non-starter. From top to bottom, the names on the list fell into one of three categories: Hear no evil, See no evil, or Evil.

There seemed to have been a very simple reality: By virtue of simply accepting a post with the president, or being one of his defenders, these individuals demonstrated an extraordinary depth of moral and ethical bankruptcy. They indelibly stained whatever reputation they may have had. And it didn't take much digging to find that few of them had come to their posts with much integrity, the Secretary of Defense being the exception, and even he was badly tarnished by his association.

The logical successor, the vice president, was out if for no other reason than he was now sitting in isolation in Guantanamo Bay for his various crimes. The same went for the entire cabinet, except for the Secretary of Defense. The Speaker of the House had revealed himself to be a quisling and a spineless dissembler, the same being the case for the Speaker Pro Tem of the Senate, who was also showing visible signs of senility.

This situation shone a harsh light on the Constitution, as did other realities that confronted the

Transition Team, not the least of which was the ease with which the administration and its allies in Congress and the Federal Judiciary had subverted it.

## CRITERIA AND DEFINITIONS

In Macbeth, the son asks, "What is a traitor?" Lady Macduff responds: "Why, one that swears and lies." Son: "And be all traitors that do so?" Lady Macduff: "Everyone that does so is a traitor and must be hanged." Son: "Who must hang them?" Lady Macduff "Why, the honest men."

The Transition Team had to solve a problem. It was not only *what* is a traitor? It was also *who* are the traitors, and how do you define those offenses that merit severe punishment? They started with a basic assumption: The criminality of the administration was so blatant and so visible to the naked eye that no claim of ignorance could be accepted.

If you were a part of the administration, you were by definition guilty of something. They rejected the argument that "I was there trying to prevent worse from happening." They posed a simple question: Why didn't you resign in protest? You had the same information that we did.

They defined a set of criteria. In Group One were those who had committed treason, who had betrayed their country, most notably to Russia. This group included the president, his family, members of the administration, those who worked in his campaign, and, surprisingly, several members of Congress.

Group Two included those who had used their positions to enrich themselves. The names of those in this group and their numbers were a big surprise, as was the scale of the corruption. Virtually the entire cabinet, as well as sub-cabinet appointees, were in this group of traitors, all taking cues from the person at the top.

Group Three were tools of various industry or financial groups, doing the inside dirty work with assurances of future compensation. They often overlapped with Group Two. Most of the Congress, both houses, Democrats and Republicans, were included in this group. And as the inner workings of Congress and the degree to which members simply followed orders from donors and lobbyists became public, even those who had long viewed the scene with cynicism were appalled.

Finally, there was Group Four, which consisted of those who had received lifetime appointments to the judiciary. The most notable of these was the right-wing extremist, the carefully groomed Manchurian Candidate, who had become the fifth far-right vote on the Supreme Court. But there were many others, even more extreme, funneled to the White House and approved by a feckless Senate, who now sat on the federal bench.

Could these appointments be considered legitimate? The Transition Team came up with an answer: No. The Supreme Court justice was called to a meeting and encouraged to resign. He refused. He was shown a file containing documents and financial statements that would be made public if he continued to refuse. He resigned. The others would go more easily, many muttering that this was not the democracy that they had known. It was hard to argue with that view.

The purge now had a defensible framework, along with evidentiary documents that, if made public, would reveal a stunning level of corruption and decay.

## THE CULTIVATION OF HATRED
## AND ITS CONSEQUENCES

The deposed president's path to power had been paved by playing to key groups' sense of victimization. As the president's chief external shill, the biggest star in the Nation's News firmament regularly stated, there are only three persecuted groups in America: white men, Christians and the wealthy.

Many in these groups were willing to wear this imaginary crown of thorns, and over time began to define themselves as victims. White men came to believe that the good jobs that they deserved had all gone to illegal immigrants and black people, and that their hard-earned tax dollars were being spent on shiftless minorities who passed their time drinking 40-ounce malt liquors.

The "Christians" saw persecution everywhere: in the teaching of science in schools and the requirement that businesses serve gay people or provide contraception coverage to their employees. Nation's News had cranked up an imaginary War on Christmas, and the ex-president had enthusiastically signed on to fight it, assuring Americans that it would okay to say Merry Christmas under his regime.

For the rich, it was the lack of appreciation for the great work they did, and the constant demands that they pay their taxes. They shared the president's sentiment when he said that he had sacrificed for his country by building a great company.

One of the clever strategies, among many, that the reactionary right used was to turn the tools of what they called the left against them. In this construct, the real hatred and racism was that of minorities against white people, Christians, and the affluent. Hate and haters became staples on the right, nowhere more than on talk radio and Nation's News.

As a ploy, used by people with low levels of self-awareness, it became almost reflexive. Black people had been put in their place; the liberals were a bunch of wimps, pussies and "snowflakes," and the immigrants were finally being kicked out. And, critically important to the president's fans, because *they* were the real victims, they could continue to see themselves as the *good* people.

This mindset produced a blind spot, one that would have profound consequences after the coup. None of these groups noticed the growing reality that, for the groups they designated as scapegoats, they, the self-perceived good people, had become genuine objects of hatred. And not hatred in the abstract rhetorical sense, but the kind of hatred that leads to horrendous outcomes.

For the Transition Team, this development posed a serious problem, one that they had to deal with on several levels. In recent decades, wars between sovereign states had declined markedly in number, while civil conflicts had become far more numerous. Several members of the team, along with those in its advisory and study groups, had experienced the horrors of these conflicts, in particular the ways in which they engulfed everyone — young, old, women, children — and not just the combatants. They had never thought of the United States in that context. They did now, and their top priority was to avoid it.

Their immediate challenge was to deal with a wave of what were defined as extra-judicial killings and attacks. In trying to understand what was happening, the team was surprised by its findings.

There were four groups that had been the administration's designated scapegoats: black people, Muslims, immigrants and liberals. The team secretly commissioned an in-depth study of post-coup attitudes and trends in these communities. The results were surprising.

With certain exceptions, black people had mentally withdrawn from active participation in society. They no longer believed any promises and held out little hope for a just society. In low-income neighborhoods, there was an appreciation of the Transition Team's promised effort to dramatically reduce levels of violence and to bring back work. But the weight of centuries of injustice, broken promises, and the levels of support for the administration's white supremacist policies may have been the final straws.

For Muslims, the coup did little to allay their ever-deepening fears about living in this country. Most came from places that had histories of military coups, none of which had ever produced a positive result.

For immigrant communities, especially Latino and Caribbean ones, the reaction was quite different. In a very short time, the administration and its henchmen, especially the neo-fascist pockets in ICE and the Border Patrol, had shown these communities that the United States was no beacon of hope or justice. It was just a larger version of Honduras or Mexico, a corrupt country where the rich and powerful always come out on top, and the poor and powerless are invariably ground down. To them the military would turn out to be just another bunch of criminals. They had seen it all before in their home countries. Better to just keep your head down and your mouth shut. Who knows, maybe it will turn out alright, at least for a while.

There were two other immigrant groups that had some worries: the rich Russians and the rich Chinese. None of them had gotten rich through hard work or grit; they were either crooks or the children of crooks, and they specialized in fraudulent real estate deals and money laundering. There were reliable accounts that the high-end real estate boom in Manhattan was financed mostly by dirty money, and that elite universities like Columbia, NYU and Harvard were floating on a sea of illegal Chinese and Russian cash. They seemed safe for now because the Transition Team had far bigger fish to fry.

Then there were the liberals. More than any of the other scapegoat groups, they had become the focus of right-wing hatred. The comments sections of on-line papers in almost any city in the country contained a daily litany of dehumanizing charges against "libtards" and snowflakes, all framed in a way that justified violence against them. Even more than blacks, immigrants or Muslims, liberals had been otherized in the extreme.

Now that their tormenters seemed to be on the run, how would liberal Americans react to the new situation they found themselves in? Would they be de-otherized?

In dealing with the criminal perpetrators, the quislings and see-no-evil groups who had engineered some of the greatest crimes in American history, would liberals remain true to their values? And to the defense of individual rights for groups they despised and who had targeted them? Would they uphold the rule of law and demand that the military government do the same? Would liberals lead the way to some form of peace and reconciliation in a bitterly divided society?

The answer to these questions came fairly quickly: No! Certain organizations remained true to their values. For example, the Southern Poverty Law Center began to track liberal hate groups who engaged in violence and assassinations. Their tracking charts became a valuable tool for the Transition Team, largely because they made clear that the extra-judicial killings were increasing in number, and that they appeared to be being carried out by well organized and highly trained individuals and groups. These groups had a clear strategy and were not about to wait for a clunky judicial system, civil or military, to swing into action.

While the nation's financial, corporate and political elites were now well protected, they couldn't be entirely shielded from the wave of assassinations that wiped out billionaires, and former billionaires, whether they remained in the United States or had gone into what they considered to be safe exile. Virtually the entire membership in the dark-money network that had financed and colluded with the administration and taken over state governments across the middle of the country was incarcerated, dead or in hiding.

And the military government seemed powerless to stop it. So powerless that the question quickly arose: How hard are they really trying? The answer to that question, which never leaked out, was: not very hard. The Transition Team had come to several conclusions, none of which they were very comfortable with.

The first was that the hatred on the part of the otherized groups for those who had actively supported or been part of the regime, was not going away. These groups were at least as important as the 30 percent, who felt, in the face of all evidence, that the coup was a terrible injustice, especially to the white, Christian and wealthy victim groups. The others' hatreds were deeper than anyone had grasped during the administration's ascendancy.

Then there was the attempt to use so-called liberal values as a hook to shape opinion and in some way defuse the situation. When asked, "Isn't it hypocritical to advocate for the rule of law for your group, and not for these others?", the standard response was either an ironic smile or "I guess it is."

Unlike Nation's News and its counterparts, liberal cable news outlets covered the wave of sniper killings, incendiary bombings and more creative murders of their former tormenters. They did not seek to justify them, but they did take an attitude of *You reap what you sow.*

The Transition Team came to a conclusion, one that was not unlike that of the post-World War II-liberation government in France. There was need for a safety valve, and this, for better and worse, was it.

When asked directly whether these semi-sanctioned killings weren't like lynchings in the American South, a spokesperson for the team responded, "Yes, they are similar, with one exception: Those lynched in the South had not committed any crimes."

Attempts to walk back this statement in the following days were not entirely successful. The cat was out of the bag, and certain groups saw the statement as a green light for various forms of frontier justice. In one of the more ironic twists, a substantial number of ostensible targets were offered asylum and a safe haven in Russia, one of the few countries where their money could buy real protection. Many accepted the offer.

In certain ways, plutocratic options were limited. First, the imposition of the wealth tax [see Part Four, "Leave Your Money and Go"] had dramatically reduced their fortunes, although they were all still comfortably within the top .001 percent. Then there was the problem of finding the countries that did not have extradition treaties with the United States. This list included garden spots like Moldova, Sudan, Uzbekistan and Yemen, not exactly the destinations of choice for this group. And, there were limits to security in places other than Russia.

The Transition Team adopted a three-track approach to managing the entrenched hatreds that now defined American society. The first was to allow the extra-judicial purge to take place, within limits, a kind of managed revenge. For example, they made it clear that any collateral damage would result in the perpetrators being hunted down and brought to justice.

Secondly, they pledged that the crimes of the administration and its collaborators would be prosecuted to the fullest extent of the law. They sent an explicit message to the Justice Department and the Judge Advocates: If you think that going easy on these people will be a good career move, you should leave now.

Finally, they began to study the biggest question: Can this country be held together? They started with a fundamental premise: Civil conflict, however it started, could only escalate, and given the fact that the country was awash in high-powered weaponry, that conflict had to be avoided at all costs.

## THE FRENCH CONNECTION

"So, sir," the prosecutor began, "let me tell you about Marshal Petain." The officers who had just overthrown their government were students of history. They knew that the military had a habit of not being very good on what to do the day after, and they didn't intend to fall into that trap. Nor did they intend to hold on to power and establish a military dictatorship.

The officers also knew that the need to restore a semblance of justice was complicated by the strong and widespread desire for vengeance, to even scores, and that many Americans felt that vengeance and justice were synonymous in the current situation.

They did their due diligence. To their surprise, it kept leading them back to 20th-century France. Like the United States in our times, France in the 1930s was a crippled democracy and a bitterly divided country. Hatreds had replaced political differences. A sense of lost greatness permeated the atmosphere. And violence bubbled just beneath the surface and often erupted in horrific clashes.

The French right had narrowed what it meant to be French to those people who looked and thought just like them, the *real* Frenchmen. A similar process had unfolded in the United States. For decades, it had become clear that when Republicans referred to the American people, they were only talking about white, conservative, Christian suburbanites. Everyone else, especially minorities, poor people, immigrants and liberals, were not *real* Americans.

Then there was the glorification of the businessman, especially the small businessman. Here the parallels were striking. From the 1930s well into the late 1950s, small businessmen — and a few women — in France were part of the base of far-right and fascist movements. They were, in their own minds, being crushed by taxes and onerous regulations. These movements invariably became xenophobic, racist and anti-Semitic. Getting rid of the others was at the heart of making France great again.

In the United States, even as the moral depravity of the administration became clear, and the empowerment of neo-Nazis and far-right street thugs became inescapable, these small businesspeople stuck with the president. Long convinced by Republican leaders that they had a special kind of wisdom, that they were victimized and overtaxed by an oppressive and incompetent government, and that they deserved to be rich, they maintained their fidelity to the regime.

While racial hatred and nativism drove much of the dynamic in the United States, anti-Semitism fueled it in France. The scars of the Dreyfus affair had never healed. And, just as the election of a black president galvanized extremist groups and those who would use them in the United States, it was the election of Leon Blum, France's first Jewish prime minister, which unleashed these forces in France. With the rise of Nazi Germany in the 1930s, there was a popular slogan on the anti-Semitic far right in France: Better Hitler than Blum. They would end up getting their wish, ushering in the shabbiest chapter in French history.

In the United States, the unstated slogan of the racist far right was Better Putin than Obama/Clinton. As the president and his inner circle of traitors consolidated power, they skillfully re-mastered Vladimir Putin's image. In just two years, Putin's "very unfavorables" among Republicans shrank from 51 percent to 14 percent, while those who viewed him favorably rose from 10 percent to 37 percent. Those numbers alarmed military leaders across a political spectrum that ran from conservative to far right.

Democratic institutions had become increasingly fragile in France in the 1930s. Fascism and Nazism were on the rise. The search for a strongman was pervasive throughout Europe. Democracy, an independent judiciary, legislatures, a free press, civil liberties? All yesterday's news, luxuries they could no longer afford. There were simple answers to all complex questions.

And all those answers led to the search for scapegoats. It worked. As the jailer in Arthur Koestler's 1940 novel *Darkness at Noon* said, "Experience teaches that the masses must be given for all difficult and complicated processes a simple easily grasped explanation. According to what I know of history, I see that mankind could never do without scapegoats."

Final tally: 40 million dead, the continent destroyed and a low point in human civilization. For France itself, defeat, disgrace and complicity in some of the worst crimes in history.

Meanwhile, in the teens of the new century in the United States, those who provided the minority of votes that put the president in office also supported the idea of a military coup in certain circumstances. In a poll, 43 percent of Republicans said that they would support such a coup. They would also get their wish, and, like the French, it would not turn out the way they had hoped, at least not for many of them.

## THE FIRST DAYS:
### *Stunning Announcements*

The first 24 hours were a day of revelations, justifications for the action taken and explanations to the public of what was coming next. The abnormal period was not going to last long, but there was no going back to the *status quo ante*. The rot was too deep and the damage done had been too great. Those responsible had to be held accountable.

The word "revenge" was never used, but it did not take a genius to figure out that many scores were about to be settled. The concept of a nation of laws had been severely undermined by the now deposed regime. It would be no simple matter to reconstruct it.

If there had been any doubt that something fundamental had occurred, it disappeared on day two, with still no word on the whereabouts of the president, vice president, key advisors, cabinet or Joint Chiefs of Staff, along with silence from members of Congress, a number of whom had been incarcerated and others of whom had been alerted that the officers had their secret financial records.

In its first major announcement, the new national leadership stunned the world. It severed diplomatic relations with Russia, ordered all American diplomats in Russia home, ordered all Russian diplomats out of the country within 48 hours, and froze Russian assets in the United States. It gave two reasons for these actions: treasonous acts by members of the administration in dealing with Russia, and continuing Russian cyber-activities that approached the level of acts of war.

In a second action, the leadership informed Switzerland and various other tax havens that they had 48 hours to transmit all secret account information on American officials and members of the financial and corporate elite to the United States. Failure to comply would result in severing diplomatic relations and immediately barring Swiss banks and companies from doing business in the United States.

When, in typical Swiss fashion, leaders asked if the matter couldn't be discussed in a reasonable manner, they received a simple answer: No.

A similar message was sent to a number of offshore tax and money laundering havens, except that they were not warned of a severance of diplomatic relations. They were told that the U.S. military would come to get the information if it weren't turned over, and that it would be a mistake to destroy the records that were being demanded.

Finally, what had been seen as one of the liberal news channels released, with authorization from the leadership, Vladimir Putin's financial records, revealing him to be the richest and most corrupt man on earth.

On day three, the same outlet released the long-hidden tax returns of the deposed president and his family members. The revealed a level of wealth far below that of Putin, as well as many American plutocrats, but a history of corruption and criminal associations going back decades, including clear evidentiary support for the belief that he had been blackmailed by Russia and that much of his fortune came from money laundering.

In another pre-emptive action, as the FBI reported activity among white-nationalist and armed neo-Nazi and extremist militias, the leaders ordered mass roundups of these groups. Their members were transported to Idaho, lodged in camps and other temporary housing, fitted with ankle bracelets with GPS and informed that they would be shot on sight if they left the state. The government that they so hated had now given them real reason to hate it. Mostly big talkers, they had played with fire, and now they were permanent residents of Idaho, the current and future white-supremacist capital of America.

## EXECUTION

The coup had been launched, and by any standard it had gone off smoothly. The entire leadership — president, his family and coterie, White House staff, Cabinet members, the Joint Chiefs (except for those who had participated in planning the coup), members of the Congressional leadership and the Supreme Court — were rounded up and taken to the Marine base at Quantico, Virginia, where they were held incommunicado. It was, to use the standard phrase, a bloodless coup.

All media outlets were forbidden to print, broadcast or release any information not approved by the Transitional Executive Committee. They were warned that to do so would constitute a capital offense. When a far-right web site with ties to the ousted administration put out a report calling for resistance, its editors and managers, including high-profile figures, were arrested and, to widespread disbelief, summarily executed by a firing squad. Once again there was a French rationale for the officers' lethal action: *pour encourager les autres.*

To win the communication and messaging war, the military had agreed upon a strategy: the sequential — hour by hour — release of documents and other information that confirmed that the country's levers of power had fallen into the hands of a group of traitors, criminals, collaborators, sexual predators and

**59**

self-seeking parasites. Although many of them wore expensive suits, the gutter had been in power.

Even cynics found the information shocking; the revelation of the internal, widely-shared knowledge of the president's insanity and feeble-mindedness, the close collaboration with top leaders in Russia, the daily coordination of messaging with Nation's News and far-right media outlets, and the surprising number of racists, white supremacists, neo-Nazis and fascists in high positions, led to a common and repeated refrain: We knew it was bad, but we never knew it was this bad.

Unsurprising was the willing collaboration of the nation's financial and corporate elites as long as it was kept out of the public eye. The surprise would have been if they had behaved differently, but there was one slight anomaly. Jewish plutocrats who had under the previous administration seen Nazism in attempts to modestly raise taxes on the wealthiest people could find no fault in an administration whose base consisted largely of anti-Semites.

A single theme tied it all together: money. But there was another related — and stunning — theme, especially in the world's oldest democracy: An advisor to the officers had told them to follow the money trail, and *the trail of dead bodies*. The coup leaders were men and women not easily shocked, but that last statement had helped push them to the brink.

At first, the inclusion of the media, financial and corporate elites in this public indictment raised a level of some concern among these groups. Then, as it became clear that this was serious and that there was more than public-relations messaging at work, alarm bells went off among those who had always seen themselves as invulnerable. They began to ask, Why are they bringing the private sector into this?

## PLANNING FOR TRIBUNALS

As the new leadership awaited the information from Switzerland, Luxembourg, the Caymans and elsewhere, a grab bag of senators, congressmen, cabinet members, White House aides and banking and corporate leaders asked to come forward to cooperate in cleaning up the mess and naming names. All offers were refused with the same statement: Your case is a matter for the tribunal.

The tribunals were a big part of the day-after plan. From previous experience — Nuremburg and the French purge, for example — the leaders knew that interest would wane quickly, and that the details would tend to become confusing. Given the scale of the crimes, they had to choose between speed and procedural justice. They chose speed.

The first step was to set clear priorities. Principle #1 was to start at the top and work down instead of using small fry to build a case against the top leaders.

Then there were the questions of scope. The administration was the easy part. From the president down, every political appointee was considered complicit. The president, his top aides, the vice president, White House staff, cabinet members and certain members of Congress would be the first in the dock.

The coup leaders struggled with the assertion by certain individuals that they had joined or stayed in the administration to serve the nation and prevent even worse from happening. Those claims were rejected; too much damage had been done, and little if no evidence of this selfless patriotism was provided.

Then, to the surprise of many, including those on the list, a second batch of indictments and roundups was launched. It consisted exclusively of the shadowy network of billionaires that had financed the president and many of his allies.

If any group had felt completely insulated from American society, a society that they largely controlled but were not a part of, it was this group. These were people who, if they were known at all, had their names on hospitals, museums and libraries. They provided the lifeblood for the cluster of right-wing think tanks that always came up with the right answers, and whose senior fellows regularly popped up on Nation's News and C-Span to promote the party line. This group defined the word "impunity."

They were people who knew that Americans enjoyed government benefits and that, therefore, if they wanted to get rid of those benefits, they had to destroy faith and trust in the government that delivered them. Over many years, they had played the long game, and they had succeeded.

They were the tiny sliver at the top, people who hated taxes not because they couldn't afford them but because their dollars might go to some public purpose. They were people for whom there was never enough, even though they couldn't spend what they had in a hundred lifetimes. That may have been the reason they invested heavily in cryogenics in the hope that they might live forever. Then there were their children, the nation's new hereditary elite, a segment that consisted mostly of highly educated, talentless, and entitled leeches.

It didn't take long for this group's most loathsome qualities to manifest themselves. Few of them were able to get beyond *Do you know who I am?* This was exactly the wrong button to push with the coup leaders, most of whom, despite having risen to the top of their profession, came from modest families, and included men and women who had grown up in poverty and seen the military as the path out of that poverty.

After a meeting at the United Nations, one of the officers observed that many buildings in New York City were named after the criminals they had in custody.

They took a tour of museums, libraries, hospitals, fountains, and cultural venues, and found it was true. At the end of the excursion, one blurted, "Sonofabitch. What are we going to do?"

Response: "Not our problem."

# PART FOUR
## WHAT HATH GOD WROUGHT?

### UNDERSTANDING PLUTOCRACY

*Military people live in a kind of bubble; they* mostly deal with other military people, and lines and hierarchies are clearly defined. There is not a lot of conspicuous wealth, and they rarely come in contact with rich people. In this last respect, they are not much different from the rest of the bottom 99 percent, who rarely see those who don't fly commercial and whose kids rarely enlist.

They are a group that prefers to glorify the military from a luxury box at ball games rather than serve in it. As a result, when the two inevitably came into contact after the coup, each realized that they had misread the other.

Those who overthrew the civilian government faced a fundamental choice. They were firmly committed to not becoming a ruling junta and were equally committed to a rapid restoration of representative democracy.

But the more they looked, the more they understood that the man they had just unseated was a symptom of something far deeper, that the system they had just replaced was not a representative democracy. The president they had just removed was not only a senile, mentally defective narcissist: He was the active tool of that tiny sliver of the population that controlled enormous wealth, so enormous that it was beyond the officers' imaginations.

After the briefest of discussions, the officers realized that the social distance between the plutocrats and the little people was so vast as to be unbridgeable. It was no exaggeration to say that these people lived in different countries, and that these countries had nothing to do with one another.

For the people who controlled that wealth, and especially those who controlled the administration, the singular measure of their value as humans was money. It was why they had contempt for the losers, the little people and, at the bottom, those who were dependent and therefore had negative value and should probably be thrown overboard. Their social isolation was so great that they were surprised that their views shocked the officers.

These people had more money than they could ever spend, and yet they cheated on their taxes and hid money in places like Switzerland and the Cayman Islands.

This situation and the choice facing them was something that most of the officers had not anticipated. They began to comprehend the meaning of the term plutocracy, and the reality that those who controlled the levers of power could not imagine any circumstance in which they would give those levers up. The plutocrats assumed that like everyone else, these military leaders had a price, that they would understand "who I am," and how the game was played. They were confident that in the end, these officers would get the picture and fall into line.

Most of the officers had not realized they lived in the most unequal society in the developed world, one where a United Nations' study found that a child born into poverty in the United States in the 21st century had little or no chance of escaping it. All of a sudden, they were given a crash course. And, as strategic thinkers, they recognized that if they simply replaced the criminal principals of the current administration, a new set of supplicants and sycophants would take their place within a year or two.

This new knowledge led them to a decision with even more profound implications than that of removing the president and his low-rent imperial court.

## PLUTOCRATS

When the military police showed up at their estates, mansions and condos early in the morning at the end of the first week, there was a universal reaction: shock, followed by *Do you know who you are dealing with?*

"Yes sir. Here are our orders. Would you like to inspect them?"

"I want to call my lawyer."

"That won't be possible at this time, sir."

Within six hours, America's far-right financing machine had been decapitated. In mid-afternoon, more than 70 men and women, including the titans of finance and a slice of the corporate elite, and four cabinet secretaries, all clad in orange jump suits and handcuffed, boarded an Air Force transport at Andrews Air Force Base, destination Guantanamo Bay, Cuba. Even the country's new leaders were stunned to learn that the passengers on this single plane accounted for more than one fourth of the entire wealth of the United States.

The plutocrats refused to acknowledge their low-rank captors. That would have been an acknowledgement that "the help" was now in charge. But when a full colonel came back from the flight deck, one of them said, "You know, this is just like the Bolsheviks, don't you?" The colonel responded, "I doubt that it will turn out the same. But sir, you have to admit, when you think about it, the Bolsheviks did have a point. We'll be landing in 20 minutes."

But then what? The officers now confronted the fundamental issue: Were they merely caretakers whose role was to restore the country to democracy, or were they to play a more substantive role, to make big changes while they were putting it back on a democratic track?

Two basic realities were in conflict. On the one hand, they knew the dangers of the military becoming very comfortable with power, and on the other, even in their brief period with that power, they had become increasingly aware of the fact that the United States had become a plutocracy and was on the way to being an autocracy.

They made a decision. As soldiers now immersed in civilian society, they were just becoming aware of the extraordinary inequality in American society, masked in their case by the glorification of the military on the part of those who would never serve. There was also the arrogance of the plutocrats in the aftermath of the coup, the sense of entitled invulnerability. But the clincher was the financial records that came pouring in from the offshore havens for dark money.

In the Swiss case, there were two tranches. After the initial demand, the leaders sent a communication to the Swiss banking authorities. It contained a simple message: "You are holding things back. Don't do that, or something bad will happen." The second tranche was even more stunning than the first.

The amounts of money were staggering, and the identities of those who were hiding this wealth cut across the political spectrum. They were sums that nobody could spend in many lifetimes, and yet they were hidden to avoid paying taxes or to mask the origins of dirty money. And this concentration of wealth went up year after year, in good years and bad.

The officers appointed a small group to study the matter. None of them had a background in finance, but all had advanced degrees in history or international affairs. They started by calling in former treasury officials and asking them to define the possible choices. Even though those with funds hidden offshore were excluded, the group was pretty homogeneous, and the officers quickly began to refer to these people as the Goldman Sachs/Citigroup guys.

They all spoke with great assurance, and a combined arrogance and lack of self-awareness about the dangers of destabilizing "the markets," of the importance of "shareholder value," and the consequences of "moral hazard." Given the coup, which they understood, (i.e., they always knew that the president was a psychotic buffoon and a pathological liar, it had just slipped their minds to say it publicly), they asserted that now, more than ever, was the time to stay the course. Stability, that's the ticket. By stay the course, they meant low taxes and further deregulation of everything in sight, especially the financial-services industry.

The officers quickly realized that they weren't the only ones who lived in a bubble.

In what could be described as an executive session after a final meeting with the Goldman Sachs/Citigroup guys, the working group came to a fundamental conclusion, which could be crudely summed up as: Screw these people.

They brought in a collection of economists, sociologists, and some union leaders who could be described as liberal to moderate. One of them was a French professor who had written a book on capitalism and wealth in the 21st century.

Unlike the labor union leaders, who were mostly useless and almost as out of touch with reality as the plutocrats, the professor and the liberal university and think-tank economists made a convincing case. They produced an economic and financial plan that would have been beyond imagination just weeks earlier, and that the plutocrats could never have imagined coming from their friends in the military.

The "bill" sent to Congress with instructions to pass it within two weeks consisted of four components: first, a one-time wealth tax of 50 percent on all fortunes over $500 million, revenue which would be entirely committed to a national infrastructure bank; second, a permanent wealth tax of five percent per year on all fortunes over $100 million; third, a progressive income tax that rose sharply after incomes of over a million and eliminated a range of loopholes, and last, restoration of the estate tax at a rate of 90 percent for estates over $50 million.

Congress, with its 535 stalwarts, could not believe that they were being told to pass this. The pill was made a little less bitter by the accompanying bill that eliminated the financing of campaigns by corporations, rich donors or self-financing plutocrats, arranged for public financing and instructed the media networks to plan to provide free time for candidate debates and outlaw 30-second spots.

(Media stocks dropped, and then plunged even further after television viewers noticed something unusual one evening. Something was missing. What was it? Then it struck them: There were no more commercials for prescription drugs or ambulance-chasing lawyers. The United States, by order of the military, had joined the rest of the civilized world.)

## EXODUS:
### Leave Your Money and Go

The outraged reaction was immediate and uniform. Those who had sought to control American society through their sometimes-ill-gotten fortunes or inheritances now wanted to leave the country. And they definitely wanted to leave with those fortunes. This was not the America that they knew, which of course was true. That was the whole point, wasn't it? So their lawyers approached the leaders to try to make a deal. None was forthcoming.

With a handful of exceptions, they were obviously welcome to leave, with two simple preconditions: first, that all of their taxes and penalties were paid, and, second, that they surrendered their passports with the understanding that they would never be allowed to return to the United States.

It was interesting to see the ease with which people who had defined themselves as the American elite, and had always been willing to wave the flag when there was money to be made and someone else's life to be sacrificed, were now content to leave a country in which, in reality, they had not lived for a very long time.

They were like the royal court of a decaying empire, Habsburgs or Russians, who were now going to live in mostly luxurious exile in London, Paris, Monte Carlo or some other resting place for the rich. Most of them had been able to successfully hide enough money so that even with the exit tax they would still be very rich. They would miss some things in the United States, some of the restaurants, their inner circle, and most of all, the power that their fortunes wielded. That was the sad part about being a rich exile.

Then there were the exceptions. They weren't going to be allowed to get off so easily. They had used their dark money to corrupt and pollute the system in ways that were so destructive that exile wasn't an option. They had financed and guided the administration. They had used their insider status to further enrich themselves. Worst of all, they had been the force behind crippling the United States' efforts to address the existential crisis associated with climate change.

Their motivation had been a simple one: greed-driven arrogance. This cohort would sit in Guantanamo Bay while the officers figured out what to do with them and informed American citizens on exactly who these people were and what they had done.

Unlike the bitter controversy over removing racist Confederate monuments and symbols, local decisions stripping the names of members of this group from hospitals, stadiums, museums, cultural centers and parks ran into virtually no opposition.

## THE MEDIA AND MORE
## BAD OPTIONS

The evil tycoons were fairly simple to deal with compared to next group, the media allies of the administration, its fascist leaders and the far-right members of Congress. Nation's News was at the center of this problem, but there were also the various on-line publications and talk radio.

As its inner workings, corruption and treason became more widely known, Nation's News was probably doomed without any action by the tribunal. With prescription medications and ambulance chasers already off the air, the flight of almost every other advertiser was almost certainly a kiss of death. Sustaining a network with ads for investing in gold and silver, protection against home invasions, and shady insurance policies wasn't a viable business model.

When its corrupt ties to the administration and various wealthy backers were revealed, and lists of its program sponsors widely disseminated, those sponsors fled at warp speed. One thing could always be said about corporate America: You always knew that they would never be there for you in the crunch. And so they weren't. Like the title of the old country-and-western song, "If your phone don't ring, you'll know it's me," the phone didn't ring anymore.

But what was to be done about those individuals who fueled racial and religious hatred on a nightly basis, who made a material contribution to wrecking the lives of millions of people and defended practices like torture, and who claimed to be news outlets when they were in reality parts of a (highly profitable) propaganda machine that had largely destroyed the concept of truth?

The coup leaders had enough of a sense of history and had seen enough suppression of press freedom in other countries to know they were playing with fire. They had also been marginally aware of the administration's attempts to muzzle press freedom in the United States, although they were surprised to find that administration-sponsored provocateurs were responsible for physical attacks on and intimidation of members of the press.

So they made a decision, a decision to employ a time-honored but within the context an innovative approach: to let sunshine be the best disinfectant. All the talking heads of the cable and broadcast networks, along with their bosses, and the major far-right web sites were invited to participate in a review of the events of the recent past. The format for the review would be a hearing, but with no legal risk to any of the participants unless they lied under oath in response to the questions.

They would be asked details about their coverage of the administration, its policies and their relationships, including monetary exchanges and blackmail. For example, the Nation's News group had, to a person, supported the practice of torture, and had described waterboarding as merely enhanced interrogation. They would now be asked if they believed what they said, and if so, if they were willing to be water-boarded before a national television audience expected to reach 250 million people.

They were also queried about ties to far-right, racist and neo-Nazi groups and any payments that they may have received from sponsors of these groups. They were repeatedly warned that the only charges that would be brought against them would be for perjury, and that therefore they all had Fifth Amendment immunity.

The vast audience viewing these familiar faces was shocked to learn that the prime-time lineup of Nation's News consisted of people with close ties to neo-Nazi and Klan groups, and that every one of them had taken money and instruction from the dark-money plutocrats.

One familiar face, a Nation's News regular, had said in a telecast that he had spent time with the president and found him to be highly intelligent and extremely well informed, and that all statements to the contrary were lies. He now admitted that none of this was true, and that in his few contacts with the former president, he thought he was crazy and suffering from dementia. His expression told it all. His statements were the kiss of death for his career.

In addition, their knowledge of a world that they claimed to understand in great depth as they pontificated was tested. In one instance, several members of a Nation's News group were given a blank map of the Middle East and asked to fill in the country names. None could do it. They were asked to name the states that were members of the Confederacy. None could do it. They were asked to name the last 10 American presidents. One of them could do it.

To many people's surprise, the mutant robotic blonde women performed better on these quizzes than the arrogant, snarky males. But not by much. And the executives who unwillingly participated revealed themselves to be as ignorant as their on-air "personalities."

Then they were asked to explain their support for various statements of the deposed president, statements that were on the face of it inaccurate or bald-faced lies. And when they sought to deflect, the moderator refused to let them off the hook, saying, "That's not an answer, and unlike your program, we have all the time in the world. Take your time."

The moderators treated these participants with a degree of respect they did not deserve, but for an audience that had never seen them unclothed and not in control, it was interesting to see a group of bullies acting like pitiful victims.

Finally, these individuals were confronted with statements they had made, and that had been unearthed, about their audience. These were people who had always been willing to make public e-mails and other private communications of their targets. Now, it was their turn. On the air, that audience was the *real* Americans, but off the air, the talking heads showed nothing but disdain for them. *They*, rather than the hated liberals, were, in fact, the elites that looked down on the little people in flyover country.

These revelations are what ruined them, and it brought back memories of Lonesome Rhodes, the folk-hero slime-ball in the film *A Face in the Crowd*, a self-proclaimed voice of the little people, who discovered that he had nothing but contempt for them. Turner Classic Movies began running the film, using the hearings as a lead-in, to huge ratings.

To many millions of Americans, it was becoming eminently clear that the president was not the only total fraud in a position of power in their country.

## ADDRESS TO THE NATION

One of the members of the leadership group was an Army colonel, Martin Casey. Casey had made himself an authority on communication. He had been part of a seminar on crisis management and had immersed himself in a book titled *The Power of Communication*. He now worked to inculcate the group in its basic principles: Words matter, words aren't enough, take your audience seriously, and capture the first-mover advantage.

Releasing documents and press releases in the first days and hours was not going to be enough; there had to be an address to the nation and the world to clarify the situation, explain in detail the motives and necessity for the action, address fears of a military dictatorship, and lay out the plan of action for the days and weeks immediately ahead.

Colonel Casey, previously largely unknown but universally defined by a single word, trustworthy, was selected to give the address. It would be seen and heard by what was, until then, the largest television and radio audience in global history.

Here is the text of his remarks:

*Good evening ladies and gentlemen. My name is Colonel Martin Casey. I am a member of the group that took the drastic action I am about to describe to you tonight. I am here only as a spokesperson and not as someone claiming a position of authority in our government.*

*My goal is to explain why these actions were taken, to describe what has happened, to inform you of the things that will happen in the days and weeks ahead, and most importantly, to reassure you that the transition back to an elected democracy will happen sooner rather than later. The officers who have taken this action are fully aware of the history of military coups and of the temptations of power. We will not succumb to them.*

*Let me start with the events that precipitated our action. It is the hope of the Transition Team that when I finish these remarks, most of those who continue to believe that the former president and his administration represented their interests and values, American values, will have changed their minds.*

*In our system, the primary responsibility for upholding the Constitution and maintaining our national integrity rests with the Congress, the courts and, to a significant degree, with a free press. If these institutions had played their roles, we would not be here today.*

*At a very early date in the administration, it became clear that the president and the members of his team did not respect our Constitution, that they were engaged in a variety of corrupt and criminal behaviors, and that the president himself was neither mentally competent nor fit to hold office. In our interactions with foreign leaders and their staffs, we were constantly told that the United States was now mistrusted and feared, and that among citizens of their countries, hatred of the United States was on the rise.*

*In reports, many of which were leaked to the press, we were told of statements and actions by the president and his inner circle that were dangerous and criminal. His indifference to human life, except his own, became inescapable, and his planned actions for using the military made soldiers, sailors and marines at every level complicit in what would be war crimes. Secret instructions had been issued to our forces to ignore any commands for a nuclear strike coming from the president.*

*In addition, the president and his team engaged in constant efforts to undermine the institutions that underpin our democracy. The president claimed that the courts were illegitimate and political, that a free press was the enemy, that the Congress was crooked when it didn't bend to his will, that those who didn't applaud him were treasonous, and that the agencies of government were all worthless and corrupt. He sought to create a cult of personality, the kind seen in communist countries and autocracies, and surrounded himself with sycophants, yes-men and incompetent and corrupt family members.*

*These things were all visible to the public, but beneath the surface, what was happening was far worse. In the Marine Corps, we have a code: Honor, Courage, Commitment. The other services have similar codes. We were being asked to violate those codes on a regular basis under this president. That had rarely, if ever, been the case in the past.*

*Honor means that we value life. But this president and his inner circle saw collateral damage as a good thing. They would say things like, "Maybe they'll get the message." When he was informed that Saudi Arabia had bombed hospitals and schools in Yemen, and that bomb and missile fragments had "Made in USA" stamped on them, the president asked, "Isn't that a good thing?"*

*The person at the top always defines a culture. Our culture of honor, courage and commitment was being corrupted. The same was true throughout the government. And beneath all of the rhetoric, the source of this corruption could be summed up in one word: greed.*

*Day after day, we were confronted with the fact that almost everything that was happening was driven by money. And to hide this fact, the president and his cohort intensified their efforts to divide Americans, to pit us against one another. This poison has reached into the armed forces of our country and has required us to make enormous efforts to counter it. We haven't always succeeded, and until now, things have gotten worse by the week.*

*At some point, several things became clear to us: The president was mentally and morally unfit to lead our nation. He had engaged in a range of criminal activities, activities that we now know extend back through his entire adult life.*

*When representatives of the armed services explained the impact of these activities and policies on the military and on society at large, we were met with indifference by the leaders of Congress, men and women who held the fate of our democracy in their hands. The Speaker of the House and the Majority Leader of the Senate, along with their lieutenants, have displayed a level of cynicism that shocked our conscience. They had far more damning information than we did, shared it with our military leaders, and still put party and personal fortune above our country.*

*In the days since we removed the president and his administration from office, we have received volumes of information that paint a picture even darker than the one that led to our action. We will release this information to the public over the next days and weeks to help our citizens understand why fundamental change is needed to restore our democracy.*

*We will also deal effectively with those foreign entities that have sought to undermine our democracy and its institutions. The most notable of these is Russia, with which we have severed diplomatic relations. Their actions and those of Americans in positions of power who have engaged in treasonous behavior cannot go unchallenged. There will be no sweeping this scandal under the rug; nor can we ignore the willful blindness of members of Congress and the complicity of certain parts of the media. There must be accountability and justice.*

*Greed and the power that comes with enormous wealth are at the heart of this story. And if it were not for the threats that the Transition Team employed to secure the information we have received, it would have remained buried, a huge iceberg of corruption resting beneath the tip.*

*We are moving ahead with plans for fair and open elections. We have established a basic principle that no member of the armed forces or recent retirees will be eligible to run for office in this initial cycle. We have not removed one grave danger just to put another one in its place.*

*At the same time, we are going to bring to justice those responsible for what has happened. In almost all cases, these were crimes committed by the rich and powerful, groups that have corrupted our institutions with the serene confidence that they would always be able to buy their way out. That will not happen this time.*

*Thank you for watching, and good night.*

Returning to the conference room where the Transitional Team had watched, Martin was greeted with applause.

Now for the public reaction: There were reports that across the country, people sat in silence after Colonel Casey finished, trying to process what they had just heard. Then there were reports of groups gathering on street corners in every city, discussing the address, many of them in tears. From the corridors of power, there was largely silence, and on cable news, even the biggest blowhards and know-it-alls seemed chastened.

The fact that it was a new day had begun to sink in. Nobody knew what that new day would bring, but they were, for the first time, coming to grips with how rotten and corrupt the old day had been. And to how entrenched the belief that nothing could change it had become. That belief was what began to give way with Colonel Casey's speech.

## FOREIGN POLICY:
### *The World on the Day After*

In the immediate aftermath of the coup, the Transition Team had held a principals meeting to assess the country's national security and foreign policy situation. Words used to describe the reaction to this assessment included "stunning" and "extremely depressing."

What was stunning and depressing was the enormous damage that had been done to the nation's standing in a very short period. Any lingering doubts that the leaders of the action may have had disappeared in this meeting.

In simplest terms, during the brief period in which he was in office, the president, his team and his enablers had transformed the United States from the undisputed leader of the world to just another big country. They had shattered the nation's reputation, squandered its good name and lost the trust of every nation on earth, save the autocracies and dictatorships that the president seemed most comfortable with.

Only because of its size and power was the United States too big to be a pariah, or in the parlance that Americans had used very loosely in recent decades, a rogue nation. Instead of being the world's policeman, the United States had become the world's bully.

Everyone in the room knew that rebuilding lost trust is a long, laborious and sometimes impossible process.

In the principles' meeting were the now ousted Secretary of State, the Republican heads of the Senate and House Foreign Affairs committees, and the heads of other key committees. They had either contributed to this calamity or had passively sat by as it occurred. When the chairman of a major Senate committee sought to defend his complicity and inaction, he had barely begun to speak when one of the officers in the room interrupted him saying, "Senator, for once in your life, for the love of God, just shut up."

The days of hypocritical "my good friend" and false comity were over. Two committee chairs were also stunned when they were given lists of committee members who would face criminal charges ranging from treason to an array of financial crimes. The

House list contained 14 names and the Senate five. Of the 19, 15 were Republicans. "Ashen faced" and "badly shaken" were terms used to describe this group as they left the session.

The officers demanded to know why the Secretary of State had allowed the State Department to be gutted and purged of its most talented people. One of the most powerful and arrogant people on the face of the earth, he had no answers and tried to place blame on the president and his inner circle of fascists and opportunists. As with his deposed boss, the buck always stopped someplace else. This would turn out to be true of almost all of the high-level accomplices.

The fact that the president had never during the course of his tawdry life shown loyalty to anyone made it quite easy for these men and women to return the favor. En masse, the rats were deserting the sinking ship. Somebody noted that it would have been almost admirable for someone, including a family member, to stand by the disgraced former president. None did.

## FOREIGN POLICY:
### *Now What?*

The fundamental question: What to do? Although the group had seen itself as transitional caretakers, they had not fully anticipated these levels of damage or the crises simmering just beneath the surface.

In long and contentious sessions, they made three fundamental decisions: They would try to rebuild the institutions of American foreign policy, starting with the State Department; they would restore damaged relations with our allies and democratic governments, and they would clearly and forcefully confront those who saw weakness or division in the situation, starting with Russia but including North Korea, Iran and others. This last would be a very dangerous process, fraught with multiple possibilities for calamitous miscalculation.

The State Department was the easiest. They started by purging all appointees of the deposed president. Once again, they were shocked by the extremism, corruption and incompetence of the people who had been inserted into high positions.

They asked former officials, the so-called elites and faceless bureaucrats who were favored Republican scapegoats, to return to public service to fill key positions. It was a very positive sign when the Department was flooded with responses from people at all levels willing to come out of retirement or from some other position to serve their country.

Next, the Russia problem. As the pieces of evidence continued to fall into place, there were multiple story lines. One related to a president who betrayed his country and undermined the nation's most important alliances and relationships. He did this for three reasons: He was being blackmailed by the Russians, who had damning evidence of financial and sexual crimes; there was the advantage that they saw in assisting him in the election (although they never actually believed that he could win); and there was the president's natural affinity for narcissistic autocracy on the Putin/Berlusconi model.

All of this would be sorted out over time by the tribunals and courts, with the likely result that the president, close family members and associates and certain members of Congress would live out their lives in prison.

There had been a deal offered to the president, an agreement to drop criminal charges if he resigned the presidency. He had rejected it at the time, just two months before the military took action. Now, despite his newfound willingness, it was too late.

Then there was the Russian side of the equation. The decision to break diplomatic relations with Russia was the most dramatic step the Transition Team had taken, and it had certainly gotten the world's attention. Along with it came a clear message to the Russian leaders: The United States was firmly committed to Article V of the NATO treaty and would take the strongest action against any aggression faced by any NATO member, including the little Baltic states.

They then issued a policy statement defining a range of cyber-actions as acts of war in the eyes of the United States and delivered a direct warning to Russia to stop its interventions in American elections. Policy was catching up with technology and the new reality.

This was a 180-degree turn in American policy, something rare in our country's history, but there was little backlash. Some on the left criticized it as warmongering, and the president's fans couldn't adjust to the new reality and said they were against being mean to Russia because..., well, they just *were*. The small handful of members of Congress who were on the Russian payroll remained conspicuously silent, knowing that their days were numbered.

Then on to the Middle East, and more drama and surprises. The administration had adopted policies, in some cases little more than impulses, that further militarized foreign policy in the region, deepened the Sunni-Shiite split, cemented the relationship with the decaying Saudi regime, sought to actively poison relations with Iran, and rewarded its right-wing Jewish donors and Christian lunatic base while continuing to pretend that there was a peace process for the Israeli-Palestinian conflict.

In the immediate aftermath of the coup, the surprise was that it was the United States' friends rather than its adversaries in the region who saw a vacuum and an opportunity to take advantage of the situation. In his dealings with the Saudis, the pathologically mendacious president had done what he often did: He lied. He had announced a $110-billion arms sale to our great ally and friend Saudi Arabia. But there *was* no deal. There was a wish list, and it became quite clear that the Saudis did not have $110 billion anyway. So, they now came calling, asking — or more accurately demanding — that the United States fulfill its commitment, but at a considerably discounted price.

Given America's role in the Middle East, the officer group was steeped in the recent history of the region. They called in the Saudi ambassador and delivered a very clear message, one that reversed decades of American policy. The message was that there would be no arms sale, and that given Saudi global financing of extremism and terrorism, if they didn't stop it forthwith, the United States would consider Saudi Arabia to be an enemy. "We are not going to look the other way anymore." There was shocked silence and panic in Riyadh.

Next in line at what had traditionally been the payout window were the Israelis. It was in their interest to pretend that the Saudi deal was real, and therefore that they were entitled to more American largesse to maintain a strategic balance in the region. Like the Saudis, they were also shocked by the response that they received: Not only would there be no increase in American military aid, but the recent commitment of huge amounts of money over the next decade was under review and likely to be dramatically reduced. It was pointed out that Israel was a rich country with a powerful military, and like the United States, mired in corruption. They could finance their own defense.

The Israeli ambassador made some veiled threats and was warned that if he meddled in American politics as he had in the past, he would be expelled from the United States.

Within 48 hours, there were statements on social media and elsewhere about the "whiff of anti-Semitism" coming from the Transition Team. Based on past experience, the team had expected this and confronted it head on. It issued a statement unlike any of the tap-dancing that Americans had seen in recent decades. It read:

> "We totally reject the assertion that changes in the U.S. position vis-a-vis Israel constitute anti-Semitism. American foreign policy reflects our nation's interests and values. Our policy does not get mailed in as instructions from Jerusalem, or for that matter, from a casino in Las Vegas. We reject the notion that the current Israeli government, the Israeli people and Jews everywhere are one and the same, and that any position that deviates from that government's desires is anti-Semitic. We would also urge the Israeli government to search its soul with respect to its silence regarding the recent administration's inaction in the face of rising anti-Semitism in the United States."

The statement did not mention that the Transition Team had demanded the immediate recall of Israel's ambassador, and that he had already left the country.

Finally, to complete the Holy Land hat trick, there was the congratulatory call from Abdel Fatah El-Sisi, the Egyptian general who had staged a coup and was now in the process of running his country over a cliff and turning it into the next Syria. He had been a fan of the deposed American president, but the idea of a military regime in the United States was even more heart-warming to him and he made himself available if the Transition Team needed any advice. He was also given the bad news that his days of feeding at the American trough would be coming to an end.

## FOREIGN POLICY:
### *Terrorism*

Like his Russian friends, the president, who seemed obsessed with fighting terrorism, in fact liked it. It provided a vehicle for mobilizing his base, undermining the institutions of democracy and consolidating his power.

To these ends, he made terrorism the most urgent problem facing the country, despite the fact that gun violence and car crashes killed immeasurably more people each year. Further, he had made it clear that "radical Islamic terrorism" was the only kind of terrorism that troubled him.

In vague terms, the president had once mentioned the value of a staged terrorist attack to create a sense of urgency in the country. If he had ever read a book, he would have understood the parallel to the Reichstag fire that enabled Hitler to maximize his power. But he had never read a book, so when, in a phone conversation, his Russian counterpart alluded to the Reichstag fire, it went over the president's head.

Through his actions, the president had made the country more vulnerable to a terror attack than it had been since the 9/11 events. His focus on foreign threats and the panacea of the Muslim ban made the likelihood of a homeland-based major terror event increasingly likely, something that those in his shrinking inner circle sensed he actually hoped for. When one of the new wave, low-level attacks occurred in New York City, he wasted no time in demanding new, draconian measures, including use of the soon to be repurposed Guantanamo Bay prison.

The president had often lied about the mess that he inherited, but this was the real terrorism mess that the Transition Team inherited, and the point at which liberals and progressives, who had become reluctant cheerleaders for the officers, now saw them in a different, more troubling light. Attorneys at the ACLU would be continuing to burn the midnight oil.

Unlike people who saw the problem of terrorism as a political issue or a club to beat people over the head with and mobilize nativists and bigots, the Transition Team saw it as a grave operational problem. Their response was a reflection of that view, one that downgraded the themes of due process and protecting civil liberties. To them the biggest civil liberty was the ability of Americans to live without fear of being attacked and blown up by terrorists, wherever they came from.

What drove their decision-making were the frequent attacks in Europe, as well as the more infrequent ones at home. In most of these cases, the authorities had known the terrorists, and it was this reality that convinced the team to move in a direction that, while making them very uncomfortable, was seen as essential to preventing future attacks.

Here was the operational problem: If there were 10,000 known radicals who had given evidence that they intended to act but had not yet done so, it would require at least 60,000 trained people to monitor their movements, and even then, there would be great difficulty doing so on a round-the-clock basis.

The team decided to lower the threshold for action. In cooperation with French, British, German and other allies, they defined a set of criteria for apprehending and incarcerating people who had not committed an act of terrorism but who had given clear evidence of an intent to do so, and who sought to recruit others.

Then the core questions: What to do with them? And what about their families? How do you correct mistakes? What about those who were U.S. citizens? These were complicated questions, with big tradeoffs. They were going to be made by men and women who, to a person, had seen conflict and suffering up close. Unlike the president and his toadies, they were not going to make these decisions from the comfort of a 35,000-foot cruising altitude.

They were also not going to repeat the nightmares of Abu Ghraib or Guantanamo Bay. They had seen the moral quagmire that the president and his team had created by unleashing the Immigration and Customs Enforcement services. They knew that the administration had been secretly discussing a huge contract with the same mercenary army that had brought shame to the United States in Iraq, an army whose CEO had close ties to the administration and had served as a secret middleman in corrupt dealings with the Russians.

They also knew that there were pockets of fascism and sadism in various enforcement agencies, and that those elements needed to be controlled and removed, rather than empowered. All of these considerations affected their decision. They came to the inescapable conclusion that the United States, and its European allies, could not in good conscience be repeatedly looking back after a terrorist attack and saying, "we knew about this guy" but did not act.

So they took dramatic action. They developed a clear set of criteria, which led to a list of 5,000 individuals in the United States who were deemed to represent a clear threat. They, along with the Europeans, reached agreement with Mauritania to receive and house large numbers of people, initially in camps and subsequently in communities to be built. The agreement represented a huge windfall for the impoverished country on Africa's western shores.

Then, in a single swift operation, they found and captured almost all of the individuals on the threat list. These men — and a handful of women — were quickly processed and transported to the camps in Mauritania. Where there were family members, they were notified of what had happened and given contact information for family assistance.

The uproar from civil-liberties advocates was immediate. It was also after the fact; the bell could not be un-rung. But in contrast to any previous actions of this nature anywhere, these organizations were given an opportunity to provide legal representation to convince the government that a mistake had been made. They were also given an opportunity to monitor conditions in the Mauritania camps and communities, and to work for family reunion where it was appropriate.

For the neo-Nazis and white nationalists on the list, the destination was the camps in Idaho rather than Mauritania, with the same provisions for legal assistance and ankle bracelets to prevent departures.

Like much of what they were doing, these actions brought them unwanted praise along with withering criticism. The domestic divisions that the president had stoked and deepened had not gone away. That was the next front on which the Transition Team had to figure out some immediate steps before scheduling elections and withdrawing.

## VIOLENCE:
### The Home Front on the Day After

*The members of the Transition Team all had* combat experience. They had all seen their compatriots, their enemies and innocent civilians blown apart and maimed for life. But the action had always occurred in a faraway place.

They had been shocked by the president's affinity for violence, both abroad and at home, but in most cases had been unaware of its viral effect on American society. They had become conscious of the infiltration of the military by racist and extremist elements and were surprised by the wink-and-nod attitudes of the civilian leadership to these potentially devastating trends for a force built on unity and trust. And then there was the danger that people highly trained in killing represented to civilian society.

The deeper they dug, the worse things appeared. In interviews with key White House staff members, several themes recurred time and again. First, there was a core group in the White House and in virtually all of the federal agencies that believed that civil war was coming, and who felt that it would be a good thing, that it would have a cleansing effect, restoring white Christian culture and crushing the hated liberals once and for all. All of these interviews revealed a checklist affinity for the qualities associated with fascism.

Then there was the racial component. During his campaign and in his inaugural address, the president had spoken of ending the carnage in the nation's inner cities. He had gone on to do exactly nothing, and he had done so for a conscious reason: They were killing each other, which he viewed as a good thing. "Culling the herd" was a familiar phrase among the White House staff.

As his base shrank, the president had increasingly shown an affinity for white-nationalist and racist elements, invariably with a subtext of violence. Tribalism, always a presence in the United States, had intensified with the encouragement of the boss and his inner circle. The more open his support, the more emboldened these groups became, measured in part by the clear upward trajectory in hate crimes across the country. Along

**100**

with this upswing, there was a clear message to law enforcement, especially to far-right sheriffs' groups, to go easy on the investigation of such crimes.

Finally, there was what the Transition Team began to call the leading state sponsors of domestic terrorism: the gun lobbies, the most powerful groups in Washington and in statehouses across the country.

They again confronted the inevitable dilemma: not what would be the right thing to do, but what they *should* do. The logical decision would be to do nothing on these issues, simply to act as temporary stewards and prepare the country for a return to elected democratic rule. The inescapable flaw in this logic was that the forces that had perverted and corrupted the system would simply reassert themselves in any election that did not address that corruption.

The team overcame its ambivalence and uncertainty by undertaking a series of actions that fundamentally changed the country, a country that was awash in high-powered weapons, consumed in hatred and closer to the brink of what would be catastrophic, group-against-group civil violence than almost anyone had realized.

The actions they took were swift and dramatic, and, given the stars on their uniforms, there was no possibility that the gun lobby would accuse them of being liberals or snowflakes. In fact, their actions shocked people across the political spectrum.

The first of these was to expose the corruption and coercion used by the gun lobby, followed swiftly by an order for the NRA to immediately cease and desist all its operations, and for all gun dealers to halt sales of any weapons, under severe penalty of law (although they could cite no law to support this action).

Then, the most dramatic action: Americans were ordered to turn in all weapons that fell within a certain definition, typically defined as military assault weapons. These were to be surrendered within two weeks to designated locations throughout the country, each manned by federalized National Guard troops. Those surrendering the weapons would be given a receipt to be sent to a federal agency for reimbursement. Failure to comply, if caught, would result in detention and trial by a military tribunal established especially for this purpose.

Next there were the militias. They were divided into two groups, those whose members had substantial military experience and a second group that were defined as "punks." Although these groups considered themselves secretive, they had all been infiltrated, and there was abundant information on their memberships and locations. A simple message was conveyed to these groups: You are out of business. Turn in all your weapons at a specified time and location. If you fail to do so, you will be met by overwhelming force, and we will kill you.

At this point, many liberals were warming to the idea of the military takeover, but the Transition Team's next actions would cool their ardor. One of the leaders, an African-American general, was not a West Point graduate, had grown up on the West Side of Chicago, and risen through the ranks. He was the driving force behind the urban-violence initiative.

He and the group working on this issue understood the complexities and the tradeoffs involved, especially mistrust of the police departments that they would have to work with. But they were determined to produce a dramatic reduction in violence in low-income, mostly minority communities. "They're killing each other" was no longer considered an acceptable reason for inaction.

They focused on gangs that had engaged in violence. These gangs and their members were all known to the police. In every city with high levels of gun and other violence, the leaders and members of gangs were instructed to appear at a police location at a specific time. They were told that they would not be arrested unless they did not appear.

When they showed up, these individuals and groups were told that they were going to change their lives. Or else. The first step was to inform all their members to turn in their firearms. Immediately. Most complied. Those who didn't would receive a home visit, a search based on a blanket warrant, seizure of weapons, and immediate arrest and incarceration without bail. The word spread fast.

That was it for the sticks. Next, the carrots. Everyone who turned in their weapons and agreed to reject violence and work toward community peace was given an opportunity to work on one of the impending infrastructure projects or provided with financial support for renewing their education.

As levels of violence plummeted almost overnight, the leaders realized two things: that many people were happy to live in a police state if their safety and security were assured, and that a lot of cops would be happy to deliver that police state. That was a major reason that so many of them had been big fans of the deposed president. As in almost every other area, the leaders found themselves dealing with extreme levels of complexity and unintended consequences.

The team also issued a warning to the cops, which included a strong suggestion to purge their ranks of those who shouldn't be armed. For the first time in memory, when the police unions howled about due process, rather than being placated, they were told to shut up and to stop defending the indefensible.

The complex process of weeding out the small minority of cops who were racists, fascists or suffering from some mental defect began in every city. In the end, it would turn out to be far more important than body cameras or any kind of training. And, coupled with the disappearance of guns on the street, interactions between police and community members, especially young black men, became less fraught. Some observers thought this initiative was the single most important thing the Transition Team had done.

With the silencing of the gun lobby and its media fans, America's weapons mania seemed to dissipate almost overnight. The politicians who had either been on the take or intimidated by the threat of a primary were discredited or no longer living in fear. The so-called white-identity militias proved themselves to be the wannabes and cowards that everyone had suspected. And, when identified, many ended up with one way tickets to Idaho.

The group that caused the greatest ongoing concern was the trained ex-military set who had bought into extremist ideologies, those who believed that the United States was in a state of moral collapse, and that it was on the brink of adopting Sharia law, or was irretrievably racist. Individuals in this group presented a significant terrorist threat, and the federal government, for the first time, made it a priority to neutralize them. For the Transition Team, this was a painful undertaking. But they did it, and in the process saved many lives.

In an important sense, the country's romance with guns and gun violence was at least souring, but in parts of the nation, there was seething anger about what was viewed as the destruction of unfettered access to every kind of weapon and the precious Second Amendment. Just as incensing to them was the unwanted message that Black Lives (actually do) Matter. And, predictably, on the other side, the television-appointed black leaders who claimed that the Transition Team was not respecting the black community. A chapter had been closed, but the book was hardly finished.

## BITTER FRUITS OF
## EXCEPTIONALISM:
*Glorification of the Military*

Just as there was a certain inexorable logic in the ascendancy of someone like the president to the nation's highest office, so was there a logic leading to a military coup. After all, every other institution had failed, and the military was the most trusted institution left standing.

Incremental change gives everyone an opportunity to adjust, to make compromises, to lower their standards and get used to the new ways. Yankee Stadium in New York City was a petri dish for this kind of change. Over time, especially in the years after the September 11 attacks, patriotic displays became obligatory vehicles for showcasing American exceptionalism. Patriotism and militarism became increasingly synonymous.

Not only were fans required to stand for the national anthem before the game, now they also had to stand during the seventh-inning stretch to honor

America, while Kate Smith sang *God Bless America*. These interludes were often used to recognize and honor a deserving American, invariably a member of the armed forces or some police organization, who were also invariably described as heroes. "First responders" had become a whole new category of national heroes. Never honored were nurses, doctors, teachers, social workers, etc., who were not seen as heroes protecting our freedoms.

Those who decided to sit out these displays, or even sought to go to the rest room, were courting trouble. Cops or security staff often blocked their path, and if they sat rather than stood, they were taunted, doused with beer, and occasionally roughed up by the patriotic fans while security people looked on.

An elderly man refused to stand during the seventh-inning stretch. A burly younger man wearing a Make America Great Again cap confronted him. "You disrespected our flag." The older man ignored him and walked away. The younger man grabbed him by the shoulder and turned him around. "I'm talking to you." The older man again turned and walked away, saying, "And I'm ignoring you." This time, the younger man spun him around and punched him in the face. The older man fell to the ground, fracturing his skull. He spent months in a veteran's hospital while the younger man, who had never served in the military, walked away and melted into the crowd. Not a frequent occurrence, but no longer a rare one.

And it wasn't just sporting events: Every holiday became a platform for "honoring the troops." At Christmas, instead of asking why they were away fighting endless and unwinnable wars, they were celebrated for their service. The Fourth of July, rather than commemorating American Independence, became just another occasion for glorifying the military services.

Naturally, all of this was done to recognize and honor "the troops" and "our great veterans," the "most honorable of professions." But if that profession was so honorable, why didn't more of these cheering crowds sign up for the experience? The question no one asked was why killing people and destroying things and places were more honorable than teaching children or curing the sick. What was honorable about war?

Needless to say, much of the military found this positive attention very attractive. Like those of the Greatest Generation, everyone likes being told how great they are, and the displays reinforced the belief on the part of those in the military that they were morally superior to civilian society. It also aligned many of them with the reactionaries and racists who pined for a lost golden age, that time when white men were unchallenged as being the best, minorities and women knew their place, and people knew better than to remain seated when Kate Smith sang *God Bless America*.

It wasn't just at ballgames and holidays. Under the now-incarcerated president, the glorification of the

**108**

military was ramped up everywhere, and the notion that veterans had been badly mistreated became received truth. So when a Vietnam veteran in Ohio complained about a welcoming ceremony for a group of immigrant agricultural workers and their families, he flashed back 50 years and pointed out that there had been no welcoming ceremony for him when he came back from his tour of duty. The ceremony for the immigrants was cancelled.

One of the many mini-turning points came when the president ordered the Pentagon to plan a huge military parade, similar to, but bigger than, the one that he had seen on a visit to France on Bastille Day. Although the ostensible reason for the parade was to "honor the troops," the president had slipped and told a White House staffer, who immediately leaked it, that, just think, they will all have to salute me. "I'm the Commander in Chief." Military leaders were appalled, but the terrifying reality was that he was the Commander in Chief.

And so it went.

## THE STUDY:
### What Happened and Why

In the rush of events and unanticipated crises that now faced them, the members of the Transition Team came to a conclusion. They — and, even more important, the country — needed to understand what had led to their actions. In part, they had to assure themselves that the removal of an American president by the military was justified, that they were more than just another military junta.

Thus, they commissioned a study, a huge study, modeled on the *Pentagon Papers*, which had sought to provide an understanding of the origins of the Vietnam War. A study group was organized under the leadership of a former general who had become a major critic of American policy and the militarization of society. No one was going to accuse the Transition Team of stacking the deck in its own favor.

The study group consisted of historians, political scientists, economists, journalists and representatives of the corporate sector. Politicians, members of the media elite, CEOs and Wall Street leaders immediately got a sinking feeling; they sensed they were not going to control the process or much like the outcome of this initiative.

The study group was given six months to come up with the answers to the following questions: (1) How did a mentally-ill sociopath with a documented record of criminality become president of the what had been the greatest democracy on earth? (2) Why did the nation's institutions fail when they were most needed? (3) Why did approximately one third of the nation continue to support the sociopath and his administration in the face of all the evidence? And (4) Were there remedies, and was there a viable path back to a vibrant democracy?

Given the assignment of a lifetime, the group, working in small teams, produced the following Executive Summary in less than three months.

## REPORT TO THE NATION:
*Crisis of Democracy*

*Introduction*

The replacement of a civilian government by military coup must be considered a seminal event in the nation's history. By any definition, it is a failure of democracy. In this document, we hope to describe the roots of this failure.

We start with two fundamental assumptions. First, the president and his criminal administration did not emerge out of nowhere; there was a historic path that led, if not to him, to someone not unlike him and his associates.

Second, blinded by a belief in American Exceptionalism, the citizens of our nation lost sight of the reality that the United States had ceased to be a functioning democracy.

*Historic Roots of the Crisis*

Western civilization has experienced three waves of social advancement. The first was the rights of man, the principle that we are citizens and not subjects. The second wave was the establishment of basic economic

**111**

rights such as the New Deal laws that said we, as Americans, do not let people die in the street.

The third wave, the one that we have most recently lived through, is, in fundamental ways, the source of our current crisis. It was the extension of those first two waves to groups that had previously been excluded, notably women, African Americans, and handicapped and LGBT people.

Throughout history, none of these gains has come easily, nor have they gone in a straight line. Each has been met with a powerful wave of reaction intended to push them back. Our crisis is the outcome of reactionary forces seeking to wipe out not only the most recent wave, to put women, black people, handicapped people and the LGBT community "back in their place," but also to wipe out the economic security gains of the past century.

The current wave of reaction began as white backlash in the 1960s, testament to our inability to get beyond our tortured racial history. As it gained strength, a strange but powerful alliance of bigots, nativists, losers in the wrenching economic changes occurring in the country, and corporate and plutocratic power became the dominant political force in American society.

For the reactionary alliance to succeed, it was essential that large numbers of white people, especially those suffering economic distress, be convinced that the source of their distress was government and previously excluded groups, rather than the plutocracy and an increasingly concentrated corporate sector.

This effort was a success for reaction, and a disaster for American democracy. A century earlier, the philosopher Alfred North Whitehead had described social progress and reaction to it in the following way: "It is the first step in sociological wisdom to recognize that the major advances in civilization are processes that all but wreck the societies in which the occur." Just twenty years ago, this warning would have been considered gross hyperbole in the United States. As events have shown us, it was prescient.

In our research, we have found that 1980 was a significant turning point, as a set of beliefs took root and led us to where we are. These beliefs can be summarized as follows:

- "The United States is exceptional, the "Shining City on the Hill," put here by God. Message: the rules and lessons of history do not apply to us.

- The goal of life in America is to get rich. There is no such thing as society, only markets, and instead of a society with a market economy, we should be a market society in which everything has a price. The measure of human worth is how much wealth you possess.

- Government is evil and incompetent, suppressing freedom and impeding the progress that the smartest and most talented people, businessmen, will make if they are unshackled.

• Taxes are theft, giving government the means to hinder progress and rewarding the undeserving at the expense of the deserving.

• Unstated but always implicit, white people are the best race, the most talented and hardest working; and it is their misfortune to have their hard-earned tax dollars go to support welfare queens and other parasitic groups.

• We are a Christian nation, the measures of Christianity being what and whom we are against.

• Nature exists to be plundered.

## POLITICAL DECAY

Our basic finding is that, over the years, the belief in American Exceptionalism served to mask the progressive decaying of our political system, its institutions and its processes.

What follows is a description of the American political system as we have found it in our times. That system cannot be described as a democracy.(Note on terminology: the study group rejects as inaccurate the use of the term "conservative" to describe certain individuals and groups. Instead, they are described as reactionary or "radical." There are also significant elements that fall within the accepted definitions of fascism.)

Here is a summary of the Study Group's findings, with a focus on the institutions of democracy:

**Rigged Election:** The election that resulted in the insertion of the deposed president and his administration into office was far more corrupt and tied to Russia than anyone believed at the time. Although we were repeatedly told that the electoral results had not been affected, this turned out to have been false; registration roles had been hacked in pivotal states, and they had changed the results.

**Undemocratic Process:** Despite losing the election by more than 3 million votes, the president was inserted into office by the anti-democratic (small "d") Electoral College.

**Anti-democratic Structure:** The United States Senate came to be dominated by senators from states with tiny populations, and to a person these senators were controlled by the fossil-fuel industry or another concentrated sector. For example, four senators from two states with a *combined* population of approximately 1 million wielded enormous power, while those from two states with a combined population of more than sixty million had none.

**Minority Rule:** In the House of Representatives, for several reasons including gerrymandered districts, the

Republican Party would appear to have a permanent majority, independent of whether they achieve electoral majorities.

**Collapsing Norms:** In an age in which one party feels that it can achieve permanent rule, it has taken steps that further debased democracy in our country. For example, possibly the most egregious, the Congress has determined that the term of a president that they oppose is less than four years, while that of one they can control begins immediately after the election.

**Money Rules:** The dominance and corrosive impact of extreme wealth and corporate power in our politics were far greater than we had anticipated. The entire makeup of the administration was engineered by a tiny group of families with extraordinary wealth and extreme political views. One of these families effectively staffed the White House and the cabinet.

**Voter Suppression/White Power:** Voter suppression laws were passed in multiple states, invariably masquerading as protections against non-existent voter fraud. Reactionary courts, except in the most egregious circumstances, upheld these laws. In every instance examined, lurking just beneath the surface was the (unfounded) fear that broadening the electorate would result in a loss of white power.

**Otherization/"The American People":** When interviewed, large swaths of American society defined the American People as white, conservative, suburban/ exurbanites, and Christian.

**Isolation of the "Political Class" and the nation's elites:** In extensive interviews with political leaders of both parties and the nation's financial elites, including those currently incarcerated or awaiting deportation, we found that the social distance between these groups and "ordinary" Americans was staggering. Office holders and former candidates displayed little understanding of life among what they referred to as the middle class, let alone the depths of poverty and deprivation in both urban and rural America.

What was surprising was the response to the Report. It was essentially, " What else is new?" The removal of the stranglehold of corporate and far-right media lies made all of these basic truths unexceptional.

## THE PURGE FINDS ITS CHAMPION

*"There are few examples in modern history of a nation's government that has been shorn off at the top by citizenry seeking revenge upon the political establishment, the social and business elite, its newspapers, writers, artists, and entertainers. This happened in France in 1944.... The French sent cabinet members, generals and admirals before firing squads or to life sentences at hard labor.*

*They purged newspapers, stage and screen stars (along with their producers, directors and theater owners)."*
*The Purge,* Herbert R. Lottman (1986)

In 1966, in a show of French defiance of the United States, President Charles De Gaulle withdrew France from NATO's military command. Like many such acts, this one had more symbolic importance than substance. Nevertheless, France remained outside the integrated command for 43 years, until 2009 when President Sarkozy announced that France was back in.

At the time, Tony Kovac was a Marine Major General with a strong background in European affairs. He was assigned to work through the details of the revived French-American NATO relationship. Kovac was somewhat of an outlier in the marines. A political liberal, he had been a force for racially integrating the Marine Corps. He also had advanced degrees in European History and International Affairs and taught at The Marine Corps War College at Quantico, Virginia.

Unlike many of his colleagues — and much of the American political establishment — Major General Kovac had great respect for the French military. He had been appalled and embarrassed by the talk of "surrender monkeys" and the replacement of french-fries by "freedom fries" in the House cafeteria at the time of the invasion of Iraq in 2003.

He was also a student of French history, especially 20th-century history. He read voraciously about the

**118**

Dreyfus Affair and the Indochina and Algerian Wars. Most relevant to the current situation, he made himself an authority on Vichy France and its aftermath. He was fascinated by situations in which people are confronted with moral choices, ones with real consequences for them and their nation. Such was Vichy France.

Like others, Major General Kovac had become increasingly alarmed and depressed by the recklessness, corruption, incompetence and criminality of the administration. Also like others, he noticed that without exception, everyone who worked in the administration, regardless of their motives, had their reputation stained or destroyed. He had more than a passing awareness of the damage that the civilian agencies were doing to American society and the nation's political system. But, again like others, it was something closer to home that pushed him over the edge.

Because of the president's cognitive decline, press conferences had become a rarity, with staged events with Nation's News "journalists" feeding him softball questions, and tweets being the preferred mode of communicating with the American people.

Even this proved risky, but at some point, the pressure to hold a news conference became too great to resist. It was scheduled to last 30 minutes, and the audience was carefully seeded with far-right and neo-fascist "reporters" who would get all the questions. It almost came off.

Twenty minutes into the press conference, the president pointed to one of the alt-right reporters, but by accident, that reporter had switched seats with another from an on-line conservative newsletter. This should not have been the disaster it turned out to be.

The reporter began, "Mr. President, care for our troops and veterans has been a hallmark of your administration." (So far, so good.) "During the previous administration, the president visited wounded soldiers, sailors and marines at Walter Reed several times a week, with no publicity, so the public knew little about it. The First Lady made eliminating homelessness among veterans her top priority and achieved great success." His question now: "Could you tell us how many times you have visited the wounded at Walter Reed, and if the First Lady has continued the initiative for homeless vets?"

The president, looking shaken, responded, "Many times," to which the reporter countered, "The staff at the hospital say that you have never been there, and those who worked on the homeless vets initiative say that it is dead in the water. Are they mistaken?" "Yes, those are all lies." The Chief of Staff stepped in: "Our time is up." The president walked off.

Then things got worse. The following day, the president, with an entourage and a coterie of reporters and cameras, went to Walter Reed to tell the patients that he thought they were *terrific*. He told a double amputee that he looked forward to playing golf with him at one the president's many courses. He criticized his predecessor and said that he was committed to cleaning up the mess at Walter Reed Hospital (without ever saying what that mess was). Worse, during these exchanges, he discernably recoiled from physical contact with the damaged bodies and souls he was visiting.

In the next days there were regular hospital visits from the president's family, all perfectly groomed and equipped with frozen smiles, along with the various minions assigned to this duty. Like the president, this was all very uncomfortable for them. The social distance between them and "these people" was far too great to bridge. While they loved war and praised torture, none of them wanted to come face to face with their consequences. Enjoying inflicting pain on those they despised, they never gave much thought to the effects it was having on those doing the inflicting, some of whom were now suffering from PTSD for what they had seen and done.

After a few days there was a dramatic development in the form of a petition that arrived at the White House. Signed by hundreds of patients, as well as by a majority of the medical staff, it was a formal request that the president, vice president, cabinet members and members of the president's family no longer visit the patients at Walter Reed.

There was no way to keep this item from the press. The storm was immediate, but like everything else in the bitterly divided country, it either deepened the hatred of the administration or was attacked as fake news by Nation's News and the administration's other allies and surrogates. It went away, relieving the president and his family of having to spend any more awkward moments sucking up to losers with whom they had nothing in common.

Possibly the greatest impact of this episode was to push Major General Kovac over the edge and into the group of coup plotters. In describing his action, Kovac said, "Last week I stood at the edge of the precipice. This week I have taken a step forward."

In the group, he would play a critical role in developing a strategy for the post-coup purge of criminals and collaborators. His unique knowledge was that he understood the thirst for revenge and how it must neither be ignored nor fully given in to.

In ways that he could never have imagined, Major General Kovac was about to play a big role in defining the future of the country, a country that he had always referred to as *my*, and now called *the*.

## THE MINISTRY OF FEAR

Military people like certainty. In general, they tend to force a false clarity on ambiguous situations such as popular sentiment, tending to identify with the Theodore Roosevelt quote, "Grab them by the balls and their hearts and minds will follow." Most of the Transition Team members were also conservatives, and they didn't like the idea of giving red meat to a new rabble. "We've got to move on," and "Won't it just spark a never-ending cycle of violence?" were typical refrains.

Major General Kovac rejected these arguments, and because he had a much stronger knowledge base, his arguments carried the day. He made the point that failure to exact revenge against Wall Street leaders for causing the Great Recession of 2008 had fueled public anger and a sense of injustice among significant numbers of citizens. If they had thrown those guys in jail, he reasoned, we probably wouldn't be here now.

He also made the point that, in cases like this, some forms of revenge *did* equal justice and could help restore a sense of trust; the belief among citizens that maybe *they* don't always get away with it. The goal was not to make the malefactors suffer (that was a side benefit, a bonus) but to satisfy a sense of justice among those who had been victimized and aggrieved by the administration, along with those who had stopped believing that justice was possible.

The link between what the crimes that had been committed and the resulting punishment should never be lost. This wasn't about blind, omnidirectional rage. For the culpable, *here is why this is happening to you* would be made very clear.

In the end, the Transition Team was in agreement and committed to a plan of action. Kovac was informally named Minister of Fear and Revenge. His formal assignment was to establish the Office of Legal Review and Rectification.

## THE PURGE:
*Management of Revenge*

Major General Kovac faced three kinds of challenges: political, legal and organizational. He took the last first and recruited a team of military and civilian prosecutors. He then had to decide where the accused were to be tried. Speed was of the essence in a culture with notoriously short attention spans.

At the same time, he was fully aware of the dangers of mobocracy, in part because he felt the desire for revenge and harsh punishments himself. He decided to use a mix of military tribunals and federal courts, now operating under revised guidelines, and requiring any judges appointed by the discredited administration to recuse themselves or resign.

Then the Office of Legal Review and Rectification got down to work. It defined categories of offenses: treason; corruption; economic and environmental crimes; human and civil rights violations; war crimes, and perjury.

The office defined its target list, starting at the top: what had come to be known as "the Royal Court" — the ex-president, family members and long-time insiders who had committed crimes, enriched themselves and systematically debased American democracy. Next were insiders, including White House Staff, cabinet members and agency appointees, whose explicit assignments were to undermine basic American values. The third tier included financial sponsors, especially the small group of ultra-rich dark-money families, fossil-fuel executives, hedge-fund managers, casino moguls and other economic criminals who had propped up the administration. In that tier also were media groups that had coordinated lies with the White House.

Next were those public officials, elected and appointed, who had systematically sought to undermine the investigations into the administration's corruption and treasonous activities.

Last were other prominent persons who had knowingly reinforced the lies that the president and the administration told. These included business leaders and religious figures. They had all assumed they would be given a pass, and that their transgressions would be forgotten. While they would not face prison terms, there was a unanimous decision that their opportunism should not be allowed to pass without some consequence.

In a nation long accustomed to the rich and powerful escaping accountability, there were several surprises, among them the names on the list of those being brought to justice. It was a Who's Who of recognizable political, corporate, financial, and media figures, exactly the groups that had made impunity a watchword of American life in recent decades.

Next, the charges. The last people convicted of treason in the United States, after WWII, were Tokyo Rose and Axis Sally. Suddenly some 40 American citizens were being charged with treason, including the former president, his immediate family members, members of the cabinet and the inner circle of secret dark-money supporters.

Some of these individuals had planned to leave the country because of the wealth tax. Now, they were told, they could not leave. In one instance, a Gulfstream 650 jet was stopped as it taxied to take off from Teterboro Airport in New Jersey. On board were the families of two of those charged with treason. The plane's cabin and hold were crammed with stacks of currency and gold.

When investigators went to these individuals' mansions on Long Island, they found secret doorways, behind which was an elaborate system of tunnels linking different estates, a fully equipped hospital, a large underground nuclear-fallout shelter, freeze-dried gourmet food supplies that would last for years, underground theaters, gyms and swimming pools, and a fully staffed cryogenic facility intended to secure eternal life for these families. One investigator described it as The Twilight Zone.

A company that organized mercenary armies provided security for this complex at a cost of many millions of dollars a year. It had close links to the administration.

Interestingly, its existence had been kept secret from the president and the Royal Court; if worse came to worst, the royal family was going to be on its own. Like everyone else, they were just pawns in a larger game. Like the president and those around him, loyalty and trust were alien concepts, and it was the final act of contempt for someone who had always been regarded as an *arriviste* and a low-class *nouveau riche* by the America's true economic and financial royalty.

All those arrested were held without bail, informed of their rights, given trial dates that were shockingly soon, and informed that all trials would be televised on the C-Span networks. They were informed that their previous lying statements would be entered into the court records and that if they continued lying, this time under oath, perjury charges would be leveled.

The biggest trial, obviously, would be that of the president, followed by those of the Royal Court, top aides and the vice president. Two surprises: The ex-president's lawyers requested a dismissal of charges against him on the grounds that he was suffering from dementia. The second surprise was that, based on psychiatric examinations, the Office of Legal Review and Rectification said that it tended to agree with that assessment. Nonetheless, it rejected the motion for dismissal, stating it was essential that the public see what had been simultaneously obvious and hidden from them in recent months. Further, it was imperative that the 30-percent base be confronted with the reality of what they were, in many instances, continuing to support.

There would be a trial. It would be public, and the president would, under oath, be confronted with all of his lies and corruption. Acknowledgement of his mental incapacity would be reserved for the penalty phase. And the cover-up of this incapacity would be evidence against the rest of the cast of characters, including the president's media champions.

The good news for those accused was that the death penalty for treason was taken off the table. The bad news was the number of those being charged with the most serious offense, and that the prosecutors were seeking life sentences without parole for some of the richest and most powerful people in the country.

# PART FIVE
## THE PURGE TRIALS

### GROUND RULES

*In planning for the trials, Kovac started with* a case study. On the morning of October 18, 1961, Parisians woke up to find hundreds of bodies floating in the Seine. The number of those massacred has never been determined. The dead were all Algerians who had held a demonstration the previous day, and the man who organized the massacre was the Paris Police Commissioner, Maurice Papon. It was not Papon's first brush with evil; he had held high positions in the Vichy government, including one where he organized the deportation of Jews in France to the Nazi death camps.

Kovac observed, "Papon was a big fish who slipped through the net. He wasn't the only one. We are not going to allow that to happen here." He went on to spell out the ground rules, the most basic of which was that being part of the administration constituted complicity in its crimes. Complicity had become a big word in the United States in the past two years. *I didn't know* wouldn't wash. Everyone knew, although few had the full picture of the scale of the crimes being committed.

They would not start at the bottom with the little fish to build cases; they were starting at the top: The first defendant would be the ex-president. There would be no deals, no plea bargains where the person got off without an admission of guilt, and there would be no special treatment for members of the military. (This last would prove to be particularly troublesome as some senior members of the administration made the case that they were, in fact, trying to save the country from the administration and the president.)

## THE EX-PRESIDENT'S TRIAL:
### *Movie Night*

For a group of military men and women, the coup leaders were an unusually diverse team. Like Major General Kovac, Vice Admiral Jack Devine had taken his own path to the most drastic action of his life. Within his circle, Devine was the first to conclude that the president's insertion into office was the greatest calamity to face the nation since the Civil War. At the same time, he was a cautious man and hoped for the best. It didn't take long for that phase to end.

Trained as a Jesuit, he had left the religious order, gone to law school and joined the Navy, where his rise had been rapid. He was the grandson of a film actor, who had instilled in him a love for movies as well as a skill in finding uses for them to make important points. That was the genesis of Movie Night, the pre-trial meeting with the legal team that would prosecute the ex-president.

Devine stood up to address his team. "We've been over this before, but let's be clear and make sure we are all aligned," he began. "This is more than a legal procedure. There is somewhere between 20 and 30 percent of the population that still supports this son-of-a-bitch. We want to convict him, and we also want to make it impossible for that group to defend him anymore. We don't want anyone looking at this to start feeling sorry for him or to think that we are persecuting him. That is already the story line among these bastards."

With that, he queued up several movie clips. The first was of General Eisenhower marching German citizens through a Nazi concentration camp strewn with dead bodies and dying people. The message was: This is what your government did. "We need to show Americans what their government did."

He then showed clips from trials in two other films, *The Caine Mutiny* and *Inherit the Wind*. The first was the trial of officers on a World War II minesweeper, who had seized command from a mentally unstable and paranoid captain. Or *was* he mentally unstable and paranoid? Message: We cannot leave any doubt, and we cannot give him an opening to generate sympathy.

*Inherit the Wind* was an adaptation of the famous 1925 Scopes Monkey Trial in rural Tennessee. William Jennings Bryan is cross-examined by Clarence Darrow, the famous defense lawyer of the time. Darrow threads a very fine line in seeking to destroy Bryan, knowing that the entire community is behind Bryan and his fundamentalist Christian views.

The ex-president's loyal base is the successor to that community. "We want them to turn against him. And we don't want an iota of sympathy for him in his situation."

And they started on all the formal trial preparations.

## THE EX-PRESIDENT'S
## PURGE TRIAL, DAY ONE
*Immigration and
Customs Enforcement*

At the start, day one of the ex-president's trial was a major disappointment for another of the largest television audiences in world history. Expecting to see the ex-president in the dock, they were instead seeing two preliminary witnesses, a senior official in the Custody Management division of Immigration and Customs Enforcement (ICE), and the former head of the Office of Government Ethics (OGE).

The reason for calling these two witnesses was to provide context for the ex-president's trial, essentially to say to the public, including the ex-president's faithful base, This is the country that we have become.

The ICE witness was the first to be sworn in.

**Court:** Sir, you are responsible for ICE custody operations in much of the Southwest, is that correct?

*Witness:* Yes, I am.

**Court:** In your detention facilities, do you make widespread use of solitary confinement?

*Witness:* We use it when it's called for.

**Court:** When is that?

*Witness:* It's decided on a case-by-case basis.

**Court:** Is there a policy statement and criteria for making these decisions?

*Witness:* I believe so, but we rely on the professional judgment of the staff on the ground. They're close to the action, and we try not to second-guess them.

**Court:** Are sexual assaults and sexual harassment of detainees by ICE staff a problem for the Agency?

*Witness:* Not to my knowledge.

**Court:** In the last calendar year, how many complaints of sexual assault were filed against ICE staff?

*Witness:* I have no idea. I'm actually more interested in protecting our borders from their sexual assailants.

**Court:** Would it surprise you to know that there were more than 500 such complaints?

*Witness:* Excuse my language, but that's bullshit. You know how these people are.

Court: No, tell me how they are. Wait...I withdraw that. How many deaths have taken place in your custody?

*Witness:* I don't know.

**Court:** Don't you maintain records on these matters?

*Witness:* Not anymore.

**Court:** What do you mean?

*Witness:* In the new administration, NARA gave us permission to destroy all those records and to not keep them anymore.

**Court:** Who is NARA?

*Witness:* It's the National Archives and Records Administration.

**Court:** And they gave you permission to destroy records of sexual assaults and deaths in your custody?

*Witness:* Yes, they had a bunch of liberals in there, but the new administration cleaned house, so we didn't have to worry about people second-guessing you every time you make a decision.

**Court:** So at this time, the numbers for sexual assaults and deaths in your custody are zero and zero, is that correct?

*Witness:* Yes, that's correct.

**Court:** Are you familiar with the Fernandez Case?

*Witness:* Can't say that I am.

**Court:** Well, let me see if I can refresh your memory, since this matter occurred under your immediate supervision. A group of Honduran immigrants crossed the border illegally in Arizona in a driving rainstorm. ICE agents apprehended them and took them to a detention center. There, the men and women, one of whom was eight months pregnant, were separated. There were seven women. They were all soaking wet. The women were told to take all their clothes by male officers and placed in a congregate detention room, naked and still soaking wet. The officers then turned up the air conditioning to high and left the women freezing in the room for the entire night. The following morning, two of the women, including the pregnant woman, were dead from exposure, and the other five were seriously ill. Now do you remember the case?

*Witness:* Sure, there was a thorough investigation, and no wrongdoing was found.

**Court:** Who did this investigation?

*Witness:* Washington sent someone down. She interviewed everybody.

**Court:** Why was there an investigation?

*Witness:* Well, the husband of one of the ones who died talked to a lawyer and started whining, so the lawyer complained to Washington, and they sent someone down to look into it. Case closed.

**Court:** Would I be correct to believe that had there not been a husband and a lawyer making the complaint, you would not have launched an investigation.

*Witness:* Probably not

**Court:** There was no disciplinary action for stripping the women naked or turning up the air conditioning, which led to two deaths?

Witness: Hey, you don't know what we're dealing with here.

**Court:** Isn't it true that the pregnant woman who died was a human rights lawyer who was fleeing death threats from criminal gangs and was seeking asylum?

*Witness:* That would still make her illegal, right?

**Court:** What happened to the others?

*Witness:* I don't know, they probably got sent back.

**Court:** A final question, with the Court's permission. Do you believe that your views are in the mainstream in your agency?

*Witness:* Not really. I'm kind of viewed as a softie, especially when it comes to the little kids. And the new guys are more hardcore.

**Court:** No further questions for this witness.

This was the beginning of the end of support by what could be called the non-fascist fringe of the ex-president's base. For many, what had been an abstraction now had a human face. Freezing pregnant women to death didn't seem like the American way. But a portion of the base was still there, and Nation's News, although crippled, had not lost its ability to appeal to the worst in people. The host of a program that night said of the dead women, "Let's not lose sight of the fact that they *were* breaking the law." She did not mention the unborn child, previously one of her favorite topics.

## THE EX-PRESIDENT'S PURGE TRIAL: DAY ONE
*The Office of Government Ethics*

There was more to come with the testimony of the current and former heads of the Office of Government Ethics (OGE). Having seen what had happened to their country's moral standing from the ICE official, they would now get a description of what had happened to government ethics in the short time that the administration had been in office. Widely noted was that the term "Banana Republic" was trending on social media.

As a young professional in the federal government, the former head of OGE had a mentor. One day, in the mid-1990s, the mentor suggested he read *Exit, Voice and Loyalty*, a book about the three choices that an ethical person faced when confronted with policies or practices that one fundamentally disagreed with, or that were unethical or immoral. "You want to be in group

**137**

one, those who exit, resign in protest," he counseled. "But don't ever underestimate the price that you will pay for being there."

OGE was a somewhat obscure office whose job it was to make sure all government employees, from top to bottom, followed federal ethics laws. These laws, while generally clear, did have some gray areas. Unfortunately, they also depended to a degree on the goodwill and honesty of the administration. It would be that dependence that would bring two OGE directors down, one through "exit," with his reputation enhanced, the other, like everyone who touched the ex-president, with his reputation — and career — in ruins.

The ex-president, his family and the inner circle all saw OGE as an obstacle and an impediment to the way they had always done — and wanted to continue to do — business. Despite his great visibility, the ex-president had never been much more than a small-time crook, and the kinds of people with whom he did business, and who were drawn to him, were similar: greedy, dishonest, and indifferent to and contemptuous of others, especially the so-called little people.

The director of OGE was one of those little people, a faceless bureaucrat. When he started to insist that those at the top follow the rules and began asking pointed questions, he became a target. The incoming administration's friends in Congress, a collection of extremists and opportunists, began to attack the director, spreading lies and false rumors about him, which were then picked up by Nation's News and the rest of the network of far-right outlets.

It didn't take a do-gooder to be appalled at the appointments that the administration was making to high positions. Even their incomplete and misleading information submissions contained profiles that OGE had never seen before. Making this information public would have provided a window into the rot at the highest levels of corporate America and Wall Street. And these were the people who would now be running the most powerful government on earth.

Even in the early months, it became clear that for this group of the already richest people, there was never enough. Grasping for more seemed to be genetically coded into their psyches. As always, the person at the top defined the culture, norms and values. What was permissible. In this case, just about anything. Just don't get caught.

The director of OGE resigned in protest as his mentor had hoped. His successor, whom he had warned against appointing, was cut from different cloth, a common type that was ambitious and pliable, a go-along-to-get-along guy. The problem was that OGE was not intended to be a pliable agency. The floodgates were now open.

And, on this day, the resigned director would testify in the treason and corruption trial of his former boss, the President of the United States.

**Court:** You were the director of OGE during what period of time?

*Witness:* I was director for the entirety of the Obama administration and the first six months of the current, .... well the administration that came in in 2017.

**Court:** Why did you leave your position?

*Witness:* I resigned for two reasons: I could not voice my concerns about the rampant corruption that was occurring from my post within the government, and I did not wish to deal with the smear tactics of the president and his staff. If they are willing to smear Gold Star mothers, just think of what they would do to an overweight bureaucrat.

**Court:** Could you compare the ethical practices of the two administrations that you served?

*Witness:* There is no comparison. The leader defines the ethical standards and values of any organization. The previous president made it quite clear that he would not tolerate unethical behavior, and his staff enforced those values. The president that you removed had no ethical or moral standards that I could identify, and he sent a clear message to his cabinet members and close associates to feel free to enrich themselves, as he and his family were doing.

**Court:** Thank you for your testimony. You are excused.

## THE EX-PRESIDENT IN THE DOCK

More than four decades earlier, many Americans had felt deprived when Richard Nixon resigned rather than face an impeachment trial. They had been right. Nixon spent the rest of his life lying and trying to rehabilitate himself, as did some of his co-conspirators, including those who had gone to prison.

With the coup, there was a similar fear, one nurtured by decades of negotiated settlements in which criminal members of the nation's financial and corporate elites skated free despite having committed egregious criminal acts. History was *not* about to repeat itself. The world was going to get a close-up look at the person who had been the most powerful man on earth.

The tone was set on day one. One thing that the Tribunal and the world would be able to immediately see in the trial was the former president's willingness to sacrifice his own family and those closest to him to save his own skin.

Many of them had shown themselves willing to return the favor. For, as it turned out, the man who professed to have many close friends actually had none. Like the Muslims he claimed to have seen celebrating the collapse of the twin towers on September 11, these friends did not exist.

The first surprise was the former president's appearance. His strange hair and orange makeup looked even stranger, and, oddly, he seemed to have gained weight during his incarceration. Most striking, his dead eyes looked deader still, a combination of soullessness and dementia. He took his seat next to his attorneys and was sworn in.

The prosecution opened with a highly unorthodox set of questions:

**Prosecution:** Sir, here is a blank map of the Middle East. Would you please put the names of the countries in the appropriate places?

*Defense:* Objection, Your Honor, this is an outrage designed to humiliate a President of the United States. This question has no relevance to anything.

**Court:** I am inclined to agree. What is the purpose of this question, and do you have other similar ones in mind?

*Prosecution:* If it please the Court, we intend to prove that the defendant was unfit to hold his office before he assumed it, and that he made no effort to mitigate that deficiency once he assumed office. These questions — and, yes, we do have others — will also demonstrate that the defendant was — and remains — a pathological liar and a criminal. This question lays the foundation for that further evidence.

**Court:** (After a pause) Objection overruled. I'll allow it.

In a shocking display of ignorance, the former president of the United States was unable to correctly locate a single country in the Middle East. In his most bizarre attempt, he asserted that the Gaza Strip was Israel. Next, the prosecution asked him to name the members of NATO. After Germany, he was lost. He was asked what the IAEA, the International Atomic Energy Agency, did. He had no idea, despite having denounced it in seeking to withdraw from the Iran nuclear deal. He was asked to define greenhouse gas. He could not. He was asked, "What is the Fourth Amendment to the Constitution?" He did not know. The 14th, the 15th? Same answer. "What is an opioid?" Response: "A drug."

Finally, he was asked to name a book that he had read in the past 10 years. "Objection!" "Objection sustained. You do not have to answer that question." The reality was, as prosecution witnesses were ready to testify, he had not read a book in his entire adult life.

After a break, the prosecution went down a new path. It read a series of quotes to the former president and asked if he agreed with them. A sampling:

"The victor will never be asked if he told the truth."

*Response:* "Agreed, that's why it's important to be a winner."

"Success is the sole earthly judge of right and wrong."

"Yes, who said that?"

**Prosecution:** "We'll come to that."

"Surely every man will have advisors by his side, but the decision will be made by one man."

**143**

*Response:* "Of course, believe me, that's true."

**Prosecutor:** "And do you agree with the following statement? 'Let me tell you, — the one that matters is me. I'm the only one that matters because when it comes to it, that's what the policy is going to be.'

"Do you know who said that?"

"No."

"Sir, you did."

"The spark of genius exists in the brain of a truly creative man from the hour of his birth."

*Response:* "This is what I have always said."

"The future will belong to the eastern nation."

*Response:* "I don't get it. "

**Court:** "Where exactly is all of this leading?"

**Prosecution:** "We have additional citations, but I believe that we have made our point. Over the years, it became a bad habit in our country to compare people with whom we disagreed to the monsters of history. For those on the political left, those with whom they disagreed were compared to Hitler. This was more or less harmless until some version of the real thing came along. We intend to demonstrate that the witness was that version of the real thing. All the quotes that he finds so admirable were from Adolph Hitler.

"The last quote, about the eastern nation, was included for a very specific reason. In many of his actions, including those that precipitated his removal from office, the defendant displayed an indifference to human life, except his own. That indicated a psychological profile that posed a grave danger to our nation, but also to millions of others in the world. It is the same mentality, and apparently the same profile, Narcissistic Personality Disorder, that has been ascribed to Hitler. These quotations and his approval of them were intended to highlight that reality. We will now move on to the next phase."

**The Court:** "Please do.

**Prosecution:** "Sir, I am going to read a series of statements that you have made, which are demonstrable lies. Please tell the Court why you lied, or if you stand by your statements, even after they have been proven to be lies."

"*Between 3 and 5 million illegal votes caused me to lose the popular vote.*" "This statement is false."

"No, no, it's true. I won the popular vote if you take away the illegals. The Commission proved it."

The Commission was an artifice consisting mostly of right-wing extremists whose assignment was to prove that 3 million illegal voters who didn't exist all voted for the former president's opponent. In the only documented case, before the Commission was abruptly disbanded, they did find an illegal voter. She was a Green Card holder who believed, wrongly, that she was eligible to vote. She had voted for the former president, not his opponent. To demonstrate the seriousness of her crime, the State of Texas gave her a long prison sentence, to be followed by deportation.

Then, out of the blue, the former president said, "I did Morania, that was an unbelievable success, believe me."

**Prosecution:** "Sir, what are you talking about?"

"Morania, the camps that got rid of all of the terrorists, Morania."

The prosecutor finally figured out that the witness was talking about the anti-terrorist program that exiled suspects to Mauritania. "Sir, the name of the country is Mauritania, and you had nothing to do with it."

"Oh yes I did, you're the fake."

**Judge:** "Move on."

Next lie by the former president:

*"So look, when President Obama was there (Chicago) two weeks ago making a speech, very nice speech, two people were shot and killed during his speech. You can't have that."* "Sir, this statement is false. There were no homicides in Chicago that day."

"That's not what I was told. It's a cesspool, especially with the blacks."

*"And there was no way to vet those people. There was no documentation. There was nothing."* "Sir,

that is a lie. The vetting process took as long as two years."

"It wasn't like mine. Mine was super-vetting. Believe me."

This went on for more than two hours before the judge intervened. "I can't take any more of this so I am calling a halt to it. You have made your point. And, sir, in addition to the other charges against you, whatever their outcome, you will certainly face a number of perjury charges based on your testimony. That is more than enough for one day. Court adjourned."

The prosecution had achieved its first-day goal, to reveal the former president as a pathologically lying, woefully ignorant narcissist, without arousing any sympathy for him. In snap surveys, even the racist base seemed to be distancing itself from him: *never really supported him, wouldn't have voted for him if I had known this*, etc.

But there was a hard-core base that stuck with him because he "stood up for the white man," and, in the words of one of his staunchest supporters, "He wasn't perfect, but he hated the niggers, and that's good enough for me."

The next day, with the global television audience growing by the hour, testimony would focus on corruption, an issue that, along with the gutting of the federal government, had fallen off the radar screen amid the daily news cycle of crises and incendiary tweets. The result would be more shock.

The first surprise of the day was a report from the bailiff that the defendant was refusing to leave his cubicle. He was outraged that the judge had allowed the questioning yesterday, referring to him as a loser, a cocksucker and a spic (even though the judge was of Portuguese heritage). The judge said, "We will proceed. I will consider the contempt charge later. Please inform the defendant of my ethnicity so that he is able to get his slurs straight."

The next witness was an economist, a tax authority and author who had tracked the former president's career from his earliest days as a businessman. The defense immediately objected, with the lead attorney stating that the witness hated the ex-president and had repeatedly smeared him over the years.

The judge asked, "Do you hate the defendant?"

"I do, your honor."

"And have you smeared him in your statements over the years?"

"I have, your honor, but only with verifiable facts."

"The witness may be heard."

"Exception!" blurted the defense attorney.

"So noted. Proceed."

The prosecution began by asking what term he would use to describe the defendant. "That is quite simple. He is a fraud," the witness answered.

"Please explain this characterization."

The witness described how the calamitous nature of the presidency was a continuation of a pattern that could be traced back to the defendant's youth, a pattern defined by criminality, failure and an obsession with winning that invariably took the form of someone else being the loser.

To underscore this point, the witness pointed to the reluctance of the defendant to name his first-born son junior, for fear that the father's name would be tarnished if his son turned out to be a loser.

This exchange provided a critical insight, that not only did he have to at least appear to be the winner, someone else had to be the loser, the humiliated loser. This behavior did not begin in the Oval Office with the incendiary tweets that were the hallmark of his tenure; he had either cheated or destroyed the reputations of virtually everyone that he had ever engaged, now including his own family.

The witness then went through a list of crimes and misdeeds, a record now fleshed out by the release of the long-hidden tax returns, the Rosetta Stone that tied all the pieces together — the criminal relationships, the Russia story in all of its grim details and the exaggerated wealth that enabled the defendant to present himself as a winner. The list of financial crimes included bribery, blackmail, tax evasion, money laundering, wire fraud, cheating vendors, perjury and false statements and drug trafficking. And, the witness noted, with slightly less compelling evidence, the use of hit men to cover up these crimes.

All of which continued through family connections and other links while he sat in the White House, beginning at the Inauguration, when the president and his family made sure to get out of the limousine in front of his Washington hotel. Documented examples of each were provided as the Court sat in stunned silence and a global television audience watched.

When the cameras panned to the defense, the former president's attorneys stared at the table. The impact of the testimony was only enhanced when the prosecution rested and the defense declined to cross-examine the witness. Court was adjourned.

Day four, and for all intents and purposes, the trial was over; the previous day's testimony of criminality and treason had been devastating. But on day four, there was another prosecution witness, a woman appointed after the coup to investigate actionable crimes committed by others in the administration.

The Court had now ordered the defendant back to the courtroom, where he refused to apologize, claiming that he had never made the statements that his own attorneys and others had heard him make. The judge made no comment and gave a barely perceptible shrug.

The Special Prosecutor's testimony was eye opening on a different level. It did not focus on Russia or the White House, but instead on what had happened to the institutions of American government. She said that her most important finding was that in a very short period, what had been one of the most honest, effective and transparent governments on earth had been transformed, agency by agency, into the operating unit of a kleptocracy.

It was no accident and no miscarriage of justice, she testified, that every member of the cabinet, significant numbers of sub-cabinet officials and virtually all the White House's assigned moles were now sitting in Guantanamo Bay. Taking cues from the White House, these officials had betrayed the public trust and, in some instances, betrayed their country for a simple reason: greed. To a person, these cabinet members and their aides' lives were built around money and the never-ending quest for more of it.

At the top of the heap were the defendant and his family, who had spent long hours discussing ways to monetize the presidency while simultaneously neglecting the business of running the nation. Based on all their inquiries, it wasn't just the defendant's indifference, ignorance or stupidity that crippled the administration, it was the lack of time available for governing after days and nights spent identifying new ways to generate income.

She wrapped up by saying that grievous damage had been done to the nation's institutions, and that more would be done if the complicity of the corporate and financial sectors in these crimes were ever to be fully exposed. The judge looked to the defense for an objection. None was forthcoming.

She continued, "The goals of the administration and those of corporate America were in perfect alignment. Make money and produce 'shareholder value.'" She provided an example of the damage: the opioid crisis, which, she posited, may turn out to be the greatest scandal in the nation's history.

"We are now approaching 100,000 deaths each year from overdoses," she began. "Its origins predate this administration, but its criminality, along with members of Congress and that of the pharmaceutical industry, dwarfs anything that we have seen before. The former president declared a state of emergency, and then, when word came that several pharmaceutical companies objected to any substantive action, nothing happened; and a supine Congress refused to reverse the gutting of the Drug Enforcement Agency. After all, reinstating and enforcing the law would have hit the bottom line and affected shareholder value at major corporations.

"Your honor, in this administration, that mentality has infected the entire government, from eviscerating environmental protections, to crooked defense contracts, to reopening the door to unscrupulous for-profit colleges that have saddled millions of Americans with unmanageable debt and useless degrees. If history is any guide, it will take many years to rebuild these institutions and, even harder, it will take an enormous effort to rebuild trust. Thank you for the opportunity to testify."

"The defense has no questions of this witness. The defense rests."

The judge instructed the jury, and they retired to deliberate.

Their deliberations lasted less than two days. The Court reassembled.

"Has the jury reached a verdict on all counts?"

"We have, your honor."

"Will the defendant rise?" He wouldn't.

"On the first count, treason against the United States of America, how do you find?"

"We find the defendant guilty."

"On the second count, enumerated financial crimes and corruption, how do you find?"

"We find the defendant guilty on all counts."

"On the third count, multiple instances of malfeasance and misfeasance in office, how do you find?"

"We find the defendant guilty on all counts."

"On the fourth count, multiple enumerated instances of perjury, how do you find?"

"We find the defendant guilty on all counts."

"Consistent with the practice of the Tribunal, does the jury, having weighed all of the evidence, have a sentencing recommendation?"

"We do your honor. It is the unanimous recommendation of the jury that, consistent with the gravity of his crimes, the defendant be sentenced to life in prison, without parole, and that his sentence be served at hard labor in a maximum-security institution."

The defendant and his attorneys appeared stunned. They had expected a Bernie Madoff sentence to a minimum-security "country club." But there was more bad news: The defendant had been willing to provide evidence against his family members in exchange for a light sentence. The offer had been rejected.

Life at hard labor was the judge's decision, the sentence to commence immediately despite the defense's stated intent to appeal.

A member of the Transition Team, the one with the background in French history, had sat through the entire trial. A reporter recognized him and asked, what the difference was between the ex-president and Marshall Petain in France, who had also, in his dotage, been sentenced to life in prison. "The difference?"

(pause) "What is the difference?" (pause) The difference is that at one point in his life," he replied, "Petain had done something good."

## THE HORROR SHOW

There is a small auditorium at Guantanamo Bay. One night, it was set up with five rows of six seats each. A group of what Americans would call high-value detainees were marched in, muttering and complaining, and took their seats. The group included leading officials in the deposed administration, the top on-camera and management team at Nation's News, a former vice president, and, finally, the deposed president himself. He was brought in last, looking disheveled and unhealthy, and sat silently in the back row. No one greeted him or made eye contact.

The lights went down and a screen lowered. The first grainy black-and-white images in the video were from the 1966 film *The Battle of Algiers*. The scenes showed French soldiers torturing Algerian suspects. One used a blowtorch on a man's chest, another connected electrodes to a man's genitals. A man was "drowned," a version of waterboarding, and others were trussed up and left hanging in painful positions.

Then the video shifted to more recent footage, preserved videos of Americans torturing terror suspects. These videotapes were supposed to have all

**155**

been destroyed, along with other records of war crimes, but someone had managed to spirit them away and hide them, awaiting the day when they would be put to use. That day had come. Unlike *The Battle of Algiers* scenes, which were accompanied only by music, these had the sounds of excruciating human pain and suffering.

The video ended, the lights came on and the screen went up. The audience was silent. Four men, all in their late 20s to mid-30s, walked in and stood in line in front of the assembled group. The man on the left stepped forward, looked at the group and said, "We are the people that you sent to commit these crimes." The former vice president, who had helped make the term "enhanced interrogation" popular, tried to hide, while the deposed president, who had championed the most violent forms of torture, appeared to be only dimly aware of his surroundings.

The man went on. "None of us will ever be the same, with a single exception. John here," pointing to the man next to him. "John loved his work and would be willing to go back to it in a minute, especially if we told him that you were all traitors." Now the group was getting scared. "I would finally say that, until two weeks ago, we were a group of five. But our fifth member committed suicide. He blew his head off after decapitating his wife. That is because of what you sent us to do, and what it did to us, and lots more like us. You should have thought of that."

The four men turned, and without another word, left the room. Now the members of the audience, tough guys and big advocates of harsh measures and torture, were visibly shaken. A couple of them muttered disparaging comments, but it was all false bravado.

A man in his 60s walked into the room with a small group of soldiers. He was in civilian clothes but had a military bearing. He stood in front of the group, did not introduce himself, and said, "They often say that people get what they deserve. You are fortunate that we have higher moral standards than to give you what you deserve." He then turned to the soldiers and said, "Take them back." He walked out without another word, and the group was led back to their cells, or, in the case of the deposed president, back to the military transport that would take him away.

## THE ECO-CRIMES TRIBUNAL

The public and the mass media were sometimes surprised by actions taken by the Transition Team in the name of the country's citizens. Possibly the biggest surprise was the creation of the Eco-Crimes Tribunal. People wanted to know where it came from, why it was such a high priority issue and who the tribunal was after.

The answers were straightforward. The impetus for the Eco-Crimes Tribunal came directly from the Pentagon. The reason that it was such a high priority was that the Department of Defense had facts, facts that had been systematically accumulated over a long period time and that had been factored into analyses that had been largely buried for political reasons. Never more than during the deposed administration, which had also sought to put a stop to the analyses.

Some of these studies were DOD specific, for example the likelihood that critical bases and other military assets, both at home and abroad, would be drowned by rising sea levels in the decades ahead. Others were more strategic, such as the finding that the horrors of the Syrian civil war were in part triggered by climate change. That study was never released. Everyone knew that, despite its validity, it would immediately be subjected to ridicule by the so-called Merchants of Doubt, their political pawns and Nation's News.

Within high levels at the Department of Defense there was a combination of frustration and growing anger at the refusal to deal with what was clearly *the* critical national defense issue. That anger rose to rage as the now deposed president, who had called climate change a hoax, filled top positions in government with deniers and tools of the fossil-fuel industry.

That industry had used tactics pioneered by the tobacco and chemical industries to buy time as cigarettes and pesticides killed millions of people. The fossil-fuel groups had been very successful in creating doubt about climate change in the popular mind; fewer people in the United States believed it was caused by human activity than in other developed countries. The industry had also bought elected officials at every level of government.

The people behind these efforts were corporate executives seeking to preserve shareholder value. They financed and controlled a vast network of front groups, lobbyists, politicians and media allies.

To their misfortune, these leaders had made a scheduling error; the future arrived far earlier than they had anticipated, even though some of their own scientists had warned of worst-case possibilities. In all instances, scientists working for international organizations, and within the Pentagon, had issued increasingly dire warnings, all of which were attacked as fear mongering and junk science by the various institutes the oil companies financed, along with Nation's News and its counterparts.

The year 2017 turned out to be the watershed, the year in which the industry moved into phase three. Phase one had been denial of the reality of climate change. Phase two had been denial of human causation. In phase three, driven by the events of 2017, the new party line was: Let's forget about causation and focus on remediation and adaptation.

Within the span of a few weeks in 2017, the fourth-largest city in the United States and its surrounding region were destroyed by a hurricane of biblical proportions, a storm that dumped amounts of rain previously unimaginable. Simultaneously, vast fires were burning in much of the West, including for the first time, within Los Angeles. Portland and Seattle, which prided themselves on their clean air and healthy lifestyle, now faced weeks in which people couldn't go outdoors because of smoke and ash from the enormous fires raining down on them.

Then, on the heels of the first hurricane, second and third ones destroyed much of the Caribbean, including the American territories Puerto Rico and the U.S. Virgin Islands. Thoughtful people, rather than accepting the usual line of "rebuilding stronger than ever," began to contemplate a region that would become largely uninhabitable as increasingly powerful storms became a regular occurrence. This possibility had not occurred to the fossil-fuel industry's leaders, or if it had, was a matter of indifference.

The National Oceanic and Atmospheric Administration tallied the costs of these events. Many billions just to restore and repair. But everyone knew that this was a bill that would not be paid because there would be no money to pay it. That money was gone, spent on the huge tax cut for the wealthy and corporations.

The administration's response had been to shower credit on itself for improvements in emergency response, all of which had been made in the previous administration. The president and his team had deemed it insensitive to discuss the link between climate change and these crises.

And, as events unfolded, it became difficult to ignore the reality that Puerto Rico and the Virgin Islands, with largely non-white populations and having experienced massive devastation, were getting the short end of the stick. That large numbers of people had died, that outmigration was increasing, that, like everything else the administration touched, the recovery effort was marked by massive corruption and incompetence, and that an organized cover-up had been launched to prevent the public from learning the truth.

Pentagon officials, whose assets were critical to the response to these events, watched the performance of the White House and the other cabinet departments in horror. Like much of the permanent government, they had written off the ex-president as being mentally unsound and suffering from cognitive impairment. But the appointments of fossil-fuels moles to top positions in EPA, Interior, Education, CIA and other agencies had been catalytic in moving them toward the coup.

At the top of what they viewed as a pyramid of evil was the fired Secretary of State, the former head of the world's largest oil company, the banker for the phony science and fake think tanks, the man who had known all along where things were going and what the consequences might be. He was the titular CEO of IBG/YBG, "I'll be gone/You'll be gone."

To some he seemed to be a dullard, a loser who had done his best to destroy the State Department. But to the environmental group in the Department of Defense, he was an arch criminal, someone guilty of crimes against humanity on a massive scale, even if many of the consequences of these crimes lay in the future. He was the man who had known all about the time bomb and denied that it existed.

It was this cohort of criminals, with the Secretary of State as the prime defendant, which moved the Defense environmental group to get the Transition Team to reinstate the death penalty for these crimes. Initially the Team was surprised by this demand and opposed it. In the end, after a lengthy presentation, they fully embraced it.

(The discovery phase in the eco-crimes tribunal had also identified a third threat, one that had been kept secret because of its explosive nature. It concerned California, and it was climate related. Contained in a top-secret report, it informed the Pentagon that in a confrontation between the federal government and the State of California, it was a near certainty that the State's National Guard and reserve units would fracture, and that large numbers of guardsmen and reservists would refuse to obey the orders of their Commander in Chief or their commanding officers. Environmental and immigration issues were at the center of these potential mutinies.)

The defendants in the eco-crimes cases were tried in groups by category. The four categories were corporate, government, media and academic/think tank.

The former Secretary of State was tried as a corporate criminal, along with other fossil-fuel executives and moguls who had led and financed the campaign against a response to climate change.

In the past, whenever corporate CEOs or Wall Street magnates had appeared before congressional committees, the same thing had happened: The most arrogant people in the society, the Masters of the Universe, those who had only the tiniest connection to the society in which they lived, were all revealed to be mediocrities or, if having some intelligence, to have personalities so warped that they were unable to mask their deformities. The Eco-Crimes Tribunal would parade these qualities before the world.

The trials were straightforward events, in part because the cases for the defense were so weak that they fell back on tropes such as *corporate culture* and the CEO operating at the direction of the board. But the evidence was incontrovertible. These men (and they were all men) knew that if the science supporting human activity as the driver of climate change were accepted, and the potential consequences understood, the actions that would be taken would greatly diminish the value of their companies and their personal wealth.

That value was based on their reserves, and those reserves would have to stay in the ground forever. That was intolerable, so they launched a massive effort to create doubt and to undermine climate science. In their final act, they infected the administration and sought to undermine all the institutions of government that could threaten their wealth.

This group had created a veritable army of deniers, the willfully ignorant. They were radicalized and largely driven by acceptance of the message that climate-change science was liberal, and liberals were the archenemies. As this army watched the televised proceedings, they remained silent, no remarks in the on-line comments sections of newspapers, no Facebook postings, no tweets.

They could not use the fake-news mantra, primarily because the damning evidence was all confirmed by their former guides and mentors, the CEOs, talk show hosts, and others, who were all trying to save their own skins.

In the past, these crimes would have been settled by corporate fines, with no admission of individual guilt, and promises of better behavior in the future. Those days were over, at least for the time being. CEOs, cabinet secretaries, media figures and others were all found guilty of crimes against humanity, and despite their pleas and those of their families, they were all sentenced to death by firing squad. A second group was sentenced to life in prison at hard labor.

On a dismal spring morning, the Tribunal issued the following statement: *Yesterday, those who committed the most horrific crimes against our nation and humanity were executed by firing squad.* A list of 31 names in alphabetical order followed. That was it.

Across the country there were shock waves. Americans wondered whether this form of justice represented Morning in America or the beginning of a dark night.

FRANK SCHNEIGER

# PART SIX
## INSOLUBLE PROBLEMS

## THE HARBINGER OF THE FUTURE
## THAT THEY MISSED

*In the two decades leading up to the coup and the* ensuing national crisis, there was a harbinger of things to come. In Texas, government and politics had come to be dominated by far-right Republican groups. The state's two United States senators were a right-wing extremist on the one hand, and a neo-fascist egomaniac on the other. Its House delegation included a mix of fascists, right-wing racists, tools of the oil industry and sexual predators.

Within the Texas Republican Party, a radical faction regularly called for Texas' secession from the United States. For some this was a case of holding your breath until you got your way, but for others there was the dream of a white-supremacist independent Texas. Over time, hatred of Washington was supplanted by hatred of California, especially after the deposed president had taken office.

During this period, something important was missed. In an obscure poll taken in a number of northern states, respondents were asked: Groups in Texas have called for their state to secede from the Union. What is your opinion? Few Texans heard of the outcome of this poll, but they would have found the results surprising. A majority of those who responded gave answers that ranged from "They should secede!" to "Good riddance."

In a sense, these respondents were willing to call Texas' bluff, tired of the constant threats and the sordid cast of characters who represented the state. But the response also contained the message that the sanctity of the Union meant far less than most people thought, that the unimaginable wasn't so unimaginable after all and that, as some were willing to say, "Maybe Lincoln should have let them go."

Now the shoe was on the other foot, and with a far-right, racist regime in Washington under the deposed president, calls for secession by Texas had virtually disappeared. Or, more accurately and portentously, they had moved west, to California. On the fringes at first, but then moving steadily toward the center as the reality of the administration's corruption and its environmental, social and immigration policies became clear.

### THE INSOLUBLE PROBLEM:
*Multiple Nations, Divisible, With....*

As the Transition Team worked through its action agenda and focused on the pathway back to representative civilian government, it kept bumping into the same problem. It had, at least for the time being, broken the back of the plutocracy, the lock that corporate America, Wall Street and the richest Americans had on the government. There had even been a certain pleasure in putting these groups in their place. But they invariably came back to a problem for which they could find no solution.

In the period leading up to the coup, rampant criminality had been on open display. The president's cruelty, mendacity, mental illness and cognitive decline were obvious to anyone willing to see, and the nation's isolation in the world had reached previously unknown levels. Only two countries steadfastly supported the president and his administration: Russia and Israel.

There had been a virtual torrent of irrefutable and damning revelations, along with the final reports that conclusively proved that the president's campaign had not just colluded with Russia, but that there had been only one campaign and that the Russian intervention had been decisive in putting him in office.

Despite all of this, the president's support had never dipped below 30 percent in opinion polls.

That was the insoluble problem. This group was not homogenous, but the 30 percent did share certain qualities. They were, except for a handful of opportunists and cranks, all white. They believed that white people were the real victims of racism in the United States, and the group included a significant number of neo-Nazis who went beyond talk and had produced a spike in hate crimes.

The one trait that extended across the entire continuum was an indifference to anyone who didn't look or think like them, the *others* who had been so deeply otherized that the 30 percent never thought of them as part of the American people. For example, although they didn't join the cry to deport the so-called "dreamers," brought to this country illegally as children, their deportation didn't really bother them much either.

For the most part, they hated and mistrusted their government, unless that government made clear in some way that it represented white supremacy and would seek to harm the approved list of scapegoats. And, finally, what bound them together, especially on the fringes, was a love of guns. Three percent of the population, all in this group, owned 50 percent of all the firearms in the country.

Although they were a decided minority, there were a lot of them. Too many to ignore. And as the Transition Team had discovered, the country had been closer to large-scale civil violence than almost anyone realized. To the Team's shock, there had actually been proponents of fomenting a race-based civil war in the White House and key cabinet departments.

The Transition Team thus came to a set of conclusions they would have never even contemplated just months earlier: They did not believe that the country could be held together. The well had been so poisoned that they could find no path forward as a unified nation. Citizens needed to understand the situation and the choices open to them, things they did not currently understand.

And finally, they concluded that peaceful separation into three territories, new nation states, was preferable to the risk of further deepening existing hatreds and of large-scale civil violence, especially given the reality of a country awash in high-powered weaponry.

## PLANNING FOR PEACEFUL SEPARATION

The Team began to think through the process for dismantling the most powerful country on earth. It wouldn't be simple, and there were few successful examples, Czechoslovakia being the only one that most of them could come up with, although, interestingly, their research told them that there was little chance that the United Kingdom would hold together for more than another decade or two.

They started with a set of principles. The first was that the differences between regions and people had reached a level at which they were irreconcilable, and that the best response was to give those in the 30 percent what they had always said they wanted. Based on electoral results, the stated policy positions of those they elected, and the activities of groups such as state Republican Parties and the League of the South, what they wanted was white control, a demi-Christian theocracy, a purge of non-white immigrants, weak government, low taxes, minimal public services, lots of guns, continued mass imprisonment and corporate control of their government.

This would be a big nation-state, encompassing almost the whole middle of the country and with a population of approximately 170 million. The two other "countries" would be coastal, provisionally called Pacifica and Atlantica. Pacifica would include California, whose growing secessionist activity had had a profound impact on the Transition Team, along with Oregon, Washington, and Hawaii. State boundaries were not to be considered sacrosanct so, for example, eastern Oregon and eastern Washington might wish to split off and join Idaho in the whitest part of the central confederation.

In the east, the picture was more complicated. It seemed most likely that several states—Virginia, Maryland and Ohio in particular—would bifurcate, with their southern regions choosing to go with the new confederacy. When residents of other conservative areas, including older white people, confronted their choices, the Team was certain they would see where their bread was buttered and choose to remain in the more liberal Atlantica. The famous old lady in Florida wanted the government to keep its goddamn hands off her Medicare, but she was also quite clear that she wanted a government that provided Medicare.

### BREAKING THE NEWS:
*The "Fact Sheet"*

_____

The Transition Team's Study Group was consistently surprised by one basic finding: The 30 percent had become so obsessed with the pursuit of fall guys and their own sense of victimization that they ignored the threats to their own wellbeing. In their zero-sum view of the world, anything bad that happened to a scapegoat group was good for them. They had successfully convinced themselves that it was always the others who were going to be screwed.

And they had always thought that in the end, their white leaders would protect them, failing to appreciate that those leaders were far more beholden to rich donors and corporate interests than they were to the little people. In large part, this belief was based on the powerful role that Nation's News had played in shaping their views, especially their sense of victimization and their hatred of liberals.

The military wasn't very good at this kind of communication, and in recent decades, it had fallen into the trap of using Madison Avenue hucksters for things like recruitment. But the Transition Team knew that how it handled this situation was critical to the future. They decided to do it themselves, no sugar coating and nothing slick.

They kept returning to a set of basic themes: The well was too poisoned, group and regional differences and hatreds too great, and the country too institutionally crippled to function as a unified democracy. Separation had to be peaceful. People in different states and regions had to make their choices (although, in fundamental ways, they already had).

Message Number One: Here is what you will be getting in the future, these forecasts essentially reflecting Republican and Democratic policy positions, based on the assumption that the two coastal countries would carry over some version of Democratic values and policies, while "Centralia," formerly mid-America, would be dominated by Republican values and policies.

The Study Group produced a chart that generated the first shock wave in the non-coastal states and, as opinion polls demonstrated, an alternative wave of support in the coastal regions: "Why didn't we let them secede a long time ago?"

The chart was created to suggest the core characteristics of the three newly established entities, and a stripped-down version was made available to the public.

| POLICY AREA | CENTRALIA | ATLANTICA/ PACIFICA |
|---|---|---|
| **Immigration** | stopped/outflow | continued/ controlled |
| **Environment/ Climate** | deregulation/weak | strong regs/ global leaders |
| **Military/ foreign policy** | increases/ militarization | reductions/ diplomacy |
| **Guns** | unrestricted | strong gun controls |
| **Human Services/ health** | low/market models | invest/healthy people |
| **Taxes** | low tax/regressive | progressive |
| **Human rights** | white supremacy | protected rights |
| **Social Security** | privatized accounts | protected/ enhanced |
| **Medicare** | voucher program | reformed/ expanded |
| **Infrastructure** | neglected/privatized | vast investment |
| **Poverty programs** | none/free market | substantial supports |
| **Govt. regulation** | minimal/"free society" | public protections |
| **Abortion** | illegal/widespread | legal/reduced |

In the vast center of the country, those places that had voted not only for the deposed president, but also for candidates who had advocated exactly these policy positions for decades, there was widespread panic. The reaction was, "Whoa — this isn't what we wanted!" Except it was exactly what they had *said* they wanted, in election after election.

And there was more. Sizeable numbers, especially in the South, accepted the package as long as it included white supremacy. The League of the South and its followers, including members of Congress, governors and legislators, were already proposing "Dixie" as the new national anthem and Richmond as the logical capital. They were not joking.

Despite having been fed a steady diet of racial resentment for decades, such ideas didn't go down so well in places like Des Moines and Fargo, even though they had been quite content to send racists and right-wing extremists to Congress year after year.

The chart had a powerful impact as people began to grasp that there were "on the ground" consequences for what had happened, and that contrary to what they had always believed, everything *doesn't* always turn out right, even for white people.

And, finally, that were to be no do-overs. Nonetheless, there was strong sentiment for a do-over, especially in the Midwest, along with a rapidly growing thirst for revenge against the political elites who had led them to this catastrophe. In a shocking development, a racist Congressman was beaten to death at a town hall meeting by his previously adoring constituents .

But It was too late to turn back.

## THREE CHOICES:
### *Protect Rights, Move People, Move Borders*

John Mlakar was an Army colonel and a member of the Study Group. He had been an assistant to General Wesley Clark during the civil wars in Yugoslavia and Kosovo. His parents were Yugoslav immigrants, and he spoke Serbo-Croatian and Slovenian.

For Colonel Mlakar, the wars that destroyed Yugoslavia were a searing experience, and he had developed a deep loathing of President Clinton for his fecklessness. Clinton had once said, in justifying American inaction, that the United States should avoid involvement because the conflict was driven by "ancient hatreds." At the time, Mlakar had said, "I can assure you that the ancient hatreds in Yugoslavia are not nearly as deep as the ancient racial hatreds in the United States."

It was this belief that convinced him of the need to avoid civil violence at all costs. He drew other parallels for the Study Group: The Serbs were the white people of Yugoslavia, convinced of their own superiority, but always defining themselves as the victims of the others. And he quoted the last American ambassador to Yugoslavia, who said, "As a victim, you have no qualms about being a perpetrator."

The other members of the Study Group and the Transition Team initially felt Mlakar was overstating things, and, after all, we're Americans, not some Balkan people; but as he continued to make his case, the group began to admit that his analysis and proposals made a great deal of sense.

Mlakar said that, in these situations, there were only a handful of choices. One was to schedule elections and hope that the old constitutional structures would hold together.

As a sign of how far their analysis had brought them, nobody in the group thought this plausible. The deposed president and his supporters and enablers had polluted the atmosphere beyond recovery. They believed it was no longer possible to enforce basic civil rights and democratic norms across all regions of the United States.

That left two choices: Move people, move borders, or both. Mlakar referred to his own experience in Yugoslavia, where, despite having been organized in ethnic republics, it had been a highly integrated country. "Imagine 40 percent of Americans being married across racial or religious lines, and you get the picture." In the end, it had not mattered, and mass slaughter had been the result.

"Don't think that we are the exception, and don't believe the crap about people voting their economic interests, especially when tribal values are at stake," he added.

Historically, the first option, moving people, had been carried out in lots of places, usually brutally. Before World War II, the western Ukraine had been 40 percent Ukrainian, 40 percent Polish and 20 percent Jewish. Today it is 100 percent Ukrainian, the result of mass slaughter, mass exodus and moving borders. Closer to home, one of the greatest mass migrations in history was the movement of black people from the South to the North as they fled white terror and oppression. And the replacement of indigenous people by whites in the American West had been achieved through a genocide that wiped out 90 percent of the Native American population.

The key here was to find a way to allow people to move voluntarily, and to provide them with financial support, at least temporarily. This would make these three new countries more politically homogeneous, and in the case of Centralia, more racially homogeneous, when non-whites fled to one of the two coastal countries as white supremacy was re-established at home.

Mlakar also saw an ongoing refugee problem for the two coastal countries as the forces of intolerance in Centralia inevitably became more entrenched and the search for scapegoats accelerated. He thought this outcome was inevitable as a result of what would be unavoidable economic and social decline. These refugees would be largely people of color, creating challenges for the coastal countries as their white populations began to fear being inundated.

Then there was the issue of state boundaries and borders. There was nothing sacred about the boundaries of the states as they existed. All you had to do was look at their current shapes, and you'd wonder, how did *that* happen?

The challenge here was greater in the East then in the West. In the West, driven by California, there was a clear logic to a four-state solution: California, Oregon, Washington, and Hawaii. The only big question here was whether Eastern Oregon and Eastern Washington would want to break off and join Idaho as part of the new central confederacy. (Mlakar doubted they would, once they looked at the realities, but the same could have been said about the Serbs and look at what happened to them.)

What about Alaska? Here, his analysis was quite simple: They are screwed. He had no solution, given the state's parasitic history and retrograde politics. Alaska would be an orphan.

In the East, the picture was more complex, particularly on the southern edges. It was a near certainty that all New England would readily join Atlantica, especially if the specter of being a permanent minority in a corporate, white-supremacist nation, post-West Coast exit, became likely. The only wild card was Maine, but their options were so limited that they were unlikely to do anything really stupid.

Then came the hard part, the states that straddled North and South. It seemed likely that several projected border states — Virginia, West Virginia, Maryland and Ohio — would split, with their southern regions joining Centralia. That would, in fact, turn out to be the case, as the notion of "economic man" was once again disproven by the power of identity and prejudice.

## THE MOST COMPLEX PROBLEM IN HISTORY

With each new level of analysis, the extraordinary complexity of the undertaking became more inescapable, as did the disastrous path that the administration had led the country down by playing solely to the 30 percent and the plutocrats.

At the same time, what also became clear was that, once a process of separation started, demographics and the hardening of attitudes would mean that there was no going back.

The Study Group and the Transition Team kept asking the same question: Can we find a way to salvage this country as a unified, democratic entity? And they kept coming up with the same answer: No.

Assuming a substantial majority would approve the separation (which polling numbers supported, especially on the two coasts), then what? For example, what about the minorities and immigrant populations stranded in a nation committed to reinstating white supremacy? They had no answers, except to plan for massive expenditures in relocation grants, and for the two coastal nations to prepare for an influx of refugees, most of whom would be former United States citizens.

Then there was the issue of outliers, the most notable being Minnesota. Politically Minnesota was a "fit" with Pacifica, but it was not contiguous and one had to consider the implications of distance and borders. Some in Minnesota wanted to explore becoming the 11th Canadian province, another good fit.

Next, what about stranded cities like Chicago, Detroit, Milwaukee and Madison, Wisconsin, those liberal enclaves that would now be trapped in a permanently reactionary anti-urban nation? No answers, just the prospect of mass migration and, once again, the challenge for the new coastal nations of absorbing large numbers of poor, minority and immigrant refugees.

Also within those migrating groups would be significant numbers of young, highly educated men and women fleeing stagnation and bigotry. An advisor to the Study Group said to expect a repeat of the Great Migration, when a vast number of African-Americans fled white terror in the South during the first half of the twentieth century.

The question of borders was a thorny one. Hard or soft? One of the United States' great strengths was its immense single market and the free movement of people, goods and services. Why couldn't that continue, with soft borders separating the new nation states?

A simple analysis led to another unpleasant truth: It would not be possible to have soft borders for one fundamental reason: guns. The gun issue had been a major element in the divisiveness that had torn the country apart. The two coastal nations would have strict gun controls, rolling back the NRA's power and obliterating Supreme Court edicts that had help turn parts of the United States into a free-fire zone. Whatever their economic impact— and it would be significant — there would be tight border controls and stiff penalties for gun smuggling.

The right-wing old lady who wanted the government to keep its goddamn hands off her Medicare was about to get her wish. While Social Security benefits would be portable across borders, those living in the Central Confederacy would get what their elected officials had long advocated. They would get a voucher and the "freedom" to buy their own health insurance on the private market. Seeing the danger of insolvency with an influx of Medicare refugees, most of whom had voted for exactly what they were fleeing, the shadow representatives of the new coastal nations demanded a five-year moratorium on anyone relocating to their countries seeking Medicare benefits.

Medicaid refugees posed a different problem. The deposed administration, to cut costs and save rural hospitals, especially those in the South, had repealed a Reagan-era requirement that emergency rooms could not refuse care to the indigent. They had also allowed retrograde states to impose a series of new requirements that were designed to drive people off the Medicaid rolls. Now poor people had begun quietly dying in the streets or, more often, out of sight in their homes. This group would not be turned away if they showed up at the border with an American passport or identification.

Another issue hanging out there was the status of the American colonies in the Caribbean and Pacific. Some southern voices, based on proximity, demanded that Puerto Rico and the Virgin Islands be ceded to the Central Confederacy. The two territories immediately demanded the right to choose through a referendum. It was a sign of the extent to which racial animosity had come to define American life that these two populations voted 90 percent to 10 percent to join the Atlantic nation.

Finally, the most complex problem of them all: What to do with the most powerful military in the history of the world, an entity that annually consumed three quarters of a trillion dollars. A military that had recently launched an unneeded aircraft carrier whose construction ran over budget by almost $7 billion; a military that sat on thousands of nuclear weapons and was demanding to spend another trillion dollars to "'modernize" these weapons, which, if ever used, could spell the end of humanity; a military that glorified "the troops," but spent more than half its budget on contractors, and, depending on how you counted, a military that was engaged in wars or some other action in more than 130 countries.

How do you divide this up? And what are the consequences for the world as we know it? Wouldn't the separation be great news in Moscow, Beijing and Pyongyang?

In one of the many sessions on this subject, Colonel Mlakar told the group to forget about the geo-strategic implications of the separation. It was a *fait accompli*, and their job was to figure out how to divide up the pie and what the relationships would be among the three militaries. His directive was, Prepare to be surprised.

A big surprise would be how little the United States' great power status meant to most people, and how much more important their daily lives, along with their animosities and hatreds were to them. "We are not that different from the former Yugoslavia," Mlakar had said, and he would be proven correct.

Quite suddenly, leaders from the South began to whistle a different tune. Within the U.S. structure, the South, always threatening secession, nullification or

# FRANK SCHNEIGER

"interposition" against a tyrannical central government, was having second thoughts as it became clear that the inflow of federal dollars to their states would end. These states had always been takers, getting far more in federal infusions than they paid in federal taxes.

The new tune echoed that of the insightful Ukrainian who declared, as Ukraine was about to break away from Russia, "We've done nothing wrong. Why must we be independent?" But they had played with fire for too long, and there was no going back now. They could have all their military bases, shipyards and other facilities. They would just have to figure out how to pay for them with economies based on agriculture and 20th century industries. And with climate change posing an immediate threat to many of these assets.

In working through the division of military assets, it became increasingly evident that each of the three nations would spend more on its military than any other single nation on earth. Each one would be a pre-eminent military power. Moreover, a critical decision had to be made with respect to nuclear weapons, especially the land-based missile systems that were mostly located in the central states. Military men like weapons, but these were aging, dangerous and of little deterrent value. They "kicked the can down the road."

Huge issues of constitutions, governance, taxes, and laws were all placed in the not-our-problem file. These would be up to constitutional conventions in each

**186**

place, and based on what they had seen, the members of the Study Group and the Transition Team had a deep sense of foreboding about what was likely to happen in the Central Confederacy.

Despite the purge and the removal of some of the worst criminal elements, they continued to be reminded of the toxic effects of everything that had gone before, of the 30 percent and its commitment to white supremacy in some form or other.

The Team's underlying frustration at not being able to get at this problem had led to a painful conclusion that that group deserved a consequence for what they had supported, and continued to support. That the consequence should be to give them what they had always said they wanted, that being the items on the chart, which spelled out the differences citizens could expect from future governments.

## REFERENDUM:
*The Quest for Peaceful Separation
and the Three-State Solution*

In the back of almost everyone's mind was the hope that, being confronted with the consequences and the gravity of their choices, majorities would pull back and opt for reconciliation. The Transition Team also knew that referenda were a terrible way to make fundamental decisions. The shadow of Britain's disastrous Brexit vote hung over them, but they could not fathom a better alternative. Among a series of bad choices, they felt they were making the least worst one.

The referendum was carefully structured to provide that choice. In a preamble booklet, widely distributed and posted on various government websites, voters were given a description of the likely nature of the government and services that they were choosing.

The booklet also predicted, however, that maintaining a unitary country would likely produce outcomes most similar to those projected for the Central Confederation, that is a triumph of reactionary government that large majorities on the two coasts rejected. And it laid out the alternative configurations: "Would you be willing to consider a union consisting of the following states....?" "Would you be willing to see your state divided for political reasons?"

There had been widespread criticism of polling operations after the 2016 elections, though nearly all of the criticism had been misplaced. Most of the polls were well within the margin of error, and none of them could have known about the instances in which Russian hackers had actually changed results in the key battleground states. Well in advance of the referendum, Russia had been warned that any interference in this vote would be considered an act of war. They had apparently taken the warning seriously, and there was little evidence of disruptive activity.

The pre-referendum polls showed surprising results. Historically, beginning soon after the American Revolution and up into the modern age, the voices of disunion had all been in the South. Not anymore. The great success of the South had been to nationalize its racist and reactionary message and to transform the Republican Party into the White People's Party. Race provided the wedge that opened the door to all the other reactionary goals, creating the plutocracy that now existed and paving the way for a mentally-challenged narcissist to have his finger on the nuclear button.

In places like Wisconsin, Michigan and Kansas, right-wing big shots with narrow interests supported separation since it would cement their permanent control over both the state and the newly formed national government. The Wall Street types were ambivalent but saw what the Transition Team had done to some of their heroes, now living in permanent exile, as a big danger sign. They too supported separation-better to get a big slice of a smaller pie than a whole pie that is out of your reach. As always, they would find ways to make money from other people's misfortune.

Then, the so-called little people. They split into three distinct groups. First, there were the 30 percenters. It's important to note that they were in fact about 20 percent of the population, but they were highly motivated by their sense of oppression and their prejudices. They were all for separation, seeing the perfect opportunity to stick it to the scapegoats where they lived, possibly even the chance to get rid of "these people" once and for all. They continued to delude themselves that their leaders would never screw them. To them, the chart was just more fake news.

Then there were those who could be described as liberals living in the reactionary states. Even if they had spent their entire lives there, they understood they might not have a future in those states if separation came to pass. The liberals were joined by minorities and immigrant groups, who also discerned that they could become refugees in the near future.

In the South, the picture was simpler and unsurprising. Many, but hardly all, white people there were willing to pay almost any price to maintain their supremacy, and, despite the best efforts of the Transition Team, they would successfully suppress the minority, immigrant and liberal vote. Here also, though, liberals began to weigh their choices in what was likely to be a future apartheid state, one where even living in urban enclaves would probably not provide a buffer against harsh realities.

It has been said that in the United States, for better or worse, ideas travel from West to East, most starting in California. The entire discussion of peaceful separation, initially laughed off as "more California liberal bullshit," had come to pass. In California, along with Hawaii and the Pacific Northwest, the percentages opting for separation were larger than anywhere else in the country. The only places the vote was even close were eastern Oregon and Washington and part of California's conservative Central Valley, and even here, separation had won.

In the East, there was a slightly different pattern. Only in all-white Maine was the vote close, and even there, a state that had twice elected a racist lunatic governor, separation won. People in Maine and other conservative pockets may not like minorities, Muslims or liberals much, but they liked Medicare and Social Security a lot more. There were similar swaths in New York, New Jersey and Pennsylvania, places where knowing where your bread is buttered triumphed over sticking it to those you don't like.

It was with the border states that things got tricky. Voters in Virginia, Maryland, West Virginia and Ohio all voted to bifurcate their states, establishing panels to define what would become both state and national boundaries. But, in each case, there were enough total votes for separation.

In the end, the two-century struggle for American unity came to an end, the unexpected outcome of the accidental insertion into the presidency of a mentally impaired criminal and his administration. Now there would be an 18-month to two—year process of working out the complex details, a process for which the only successful example was the Czech-Slovak one, along with the cautionary tale of British regret and deepened divisions after the first Brexit vote, which had led to increasing calls for a do-over.

A corps of what they named Wise Men was established by the Transition Team, tasked with developing guidelines for the convening of three constitutional conventions, and including the formation of criteria for the selection of national capitals, a step that was viewed as essential to stave off a bidding war akin to the competition for hosting the Olympics.

The world looked on in awe and some trepidation (although there were big smiles in a few foreign capitals) as the most complex process and set of negotiations in history got underway. The great achievement was that the transition was peaceful, at least for now.

## THE HISTORIANS WEIGH IN

Napoleon and the 18th Brumaire, Pinochet in Chile, the generals in Myanmar, Franco in Spain, and the Argentine junta and its innocently named National Reorganization Process, better known as the Dirty War, was a list on which, from the first day, the officer's group was intent on never finding itself.

They openly addressed the seduction of power and its disastrous consequences over the course of history. They kept the transition on track.

The members of the Transition Team, the coup leaders and all others who had come aboard, were aware that there was always a good chance they would spend the rest of their lives in the stockade, their families reviled and reduced to poverty. They took that risk. In addition to considering their futures, they wanted to know about their place in history, a place they would assuredly have. They needed to understand two things: Had they done the right thing? And, What had been their alternatives?

The Team assembled a panel of eminent historians and asked that first, crucial question: Did we do the right thing?

The panel gave a simple answer: "Call us back in 30 years, and we'll give you an opinion."

They *were* willing to say that what had just come to pass was the culmination of issues, trends and cycles that went back to the birth of the Republic, and which had greatly accelerated in recent decades. While the deposed president's placement into office may have been an accident, it was in some ways an accident that was bound to happen. In a first swipe at the religion of American exceptionalism, they noted that Americans had never been willing to take a hard look at their founding myths.

Especially in the downplaying of the evils of race-based slavery, segregation and genocide, white

Americans largely bought into a crocked history in which slavery ended in 1865, and a few loose ends were tied up with the Civil Rights acts of the 1960s. Redacted were the unpleasant facts that a form of slavery was reinstituted soon after Reconstruction and reinforced by white terror, and that the conquest of the West was a story of genocide against indigenous peoples.

What the historians described as profoundly troubling was the fact that the ousted administration had included numerous individuals who were out-and-out racists, white supremacists and, in some instances, neo-Nazis. And that the deposed president had been very sympathetic to their views. Americans had a habit of referring to governments that they didn't like as "regimes." The ousted administration had been a regime.

For large stretches of the 19th, 20th and now the first part of the 21st century, the country was controlled by groups of moguls, the first and second gilded ages. In each era, they were held up as extraordinary people with exceptional qualities, only to be revealed as grasping, greedy mediocrities, although blessed with, in some instances, high-order computational skills.

The modern reactionary period had produced the most unequal nation in the developed world, and the society with the least upward mobility. Historically, it was rare for situations like this to be resolved non-violently. That, in the aftermath of the coup, they had

**194**

gotten this far with so little violence was considered a historic achievement.

Through it all, the nation was never able to confront these realities. It never had a truth-and-reconciliation movement, because there was never a willingness on the part of the white majority to confront reality, or on the part of the most prominent minority leaders to skip an opportunity to score some points. And, the nation's mass media, except for the extreme right, was obsessed with balance and hewing to a middle path, even though the middle had moved further and further to the right.

Then, the true disaster, as inequality increased, and work disappeared, the Republican Party, now fully under plutocratic control and on the way to becoming the White People's Party, began to convince its constituents that they were the true victims of racism in the United States. As a result, a large portion of the white population began to display all the malignant qualities of the self-defined oppressed.

The second question, about the alternatives, had another easy answer: There are always alternatives; there are no inevitabilities in history. But, to take a counterfactual approach, the historians asked what would have happened if this group of officers had *not* acted? I What if they had allowed the administration to continue on its course of reinforcing corporate control and stoking the hatred of scapegoat groups?

To do so, the reactionary elites had to mobilize the masses to win elections. These groups were white and resentful, and keeping them mobilized meant constantly stoking those resentments.

As President Kennedy said, "Those who foolishly sought power by riding the back of the tiger ended up inside." The process had gotten out of hand, and the madman had gotten into the oval office. He posed such a grave danger to the country and the world that he had to be removed. But the rot went so deep that the system couldn't react.

The damage that was done should not be underestimated, an eminent historian said. '"Look around. Look at what happened. And try to see this entire process, the breakup into three separate countries, and an outcome that is offloading all that wreckage onto one of the three. What do you think the future of the Central Confederacy is? Do you see a democratic future? Do you see the protection of civil rights? What is going to happen to its cities? It seems to me that you have plowed all of the reasons that you overthrew the administration into one place."

He continued: "Could the country have been held together? If you think of the period of the 1850s, the country was clearly on the path to disunion, but few people saw it, and there were various attempts to patch things up to keep it together. In the period after the

Civil War, there were also similarities to our times, especially when you think of the combination of the restoration of white supremacy and the extraordinary inequality of the first Gilded Age.

"The genius of Republicans was in convincing white people that it was minorities and immigrants who were responsible for their decline, rather than plutocrats, globalization, changes in technology and the concentrated corporate sectors that screwed them year after year."

"At some point, it got out of control, but all the structures, financing mechanisms and communications systems remained in place. So, we believe that the alternative to what you have done was probably a white supremacist, quasi-theocratic, plutocratic autocracy, built on the need for a constant search for new scapegoats."

"For these powerful groups, as you saw, simply getting rid of the doddering narcissist and replacing him with a more presentable reactionary, like the extremist vice president or the pliable Speaker of the House, would have been an ideal solution. But the need for scapegoats would never go away, even after the scapegoats did."

"Finally, what the historians found was that the 50-year reactionary movement that started with white backlash had reached its end stage, now seeking to reverse gains made by women, minorities, LGBT people and immigrants, along with the social gains going back to the New Deal. Even those with disabilities, previously exempted from scapegoat designation, were now on the firing line, as a radicalized Congress sought to gut the Americans with Disabilities Act.

Once again, as Alfred North Whitehead said a century ago, the processes for achieving social progress had produced reactions that all but wreck the societies in which they occur. The final note: Look around. Survey the wreckage. Don't let our misplaced belief in American exceptionalism blind you to reality."

# PART SEVEN
## A LOOK BACK

## AFTER THE DUST SETTLED

*Many of those convicted of serious crimes received* long sentences, typically at hard labor, as opposed to the white-collar prisons they had expected. Some complained that Bernie Madoff was getting special treatment compared to their harsh conditions.

Most of these prisons were in the eastern part of the former United States. In one of its final acts, the Transition Team had closed Guantanamo Bay and ceded the area back to Cuba. In a gesture of goodwill, the Cubans sent a check for $236,930, rebating 58 years of American rent payments, $4,085 per year, checks that had never been cashed anyway.

Over time, those imprisoned saw an opportunity for release by being transferred to institutions in the recently formed Central Confederacy, a/k/a Centralia. These applications were mostly granted, and soon men and women began to be paroled after having served less than half of their sentences.

Now what? There had been talk of reconciliation among the newly formed countries, but these seeds had fallen on barren ground. The poisonous atmosphere of the last years of the United States was still too fresh. All of those released were deemed *persona non-grata* in the two coastal nations. Some chose to start over abroad, but the number of countries willing to antagonize either Atlantica or Pacifica by accepting them was limited to the now entrenched racist regimes of East Central Europe and, in a few cases, Israel.

Those who had been the media voices of fascism and white power found it particularly tough sledding. In their trials they had been revealed, almost without exception, to be sniveling cowards, know-nothings and pathological liars. And anyway, in a country in which white supremacy was now official policy, the old Nation's News crowd wasn't needed for flame fanning any more.

Then there were the politicians who had actively sought to wreck the country while enriching themselves. They fared a little better, although their performances at trial were as unflattering as those of the talking heads. Posturing blowhards, always willing to abuse a defenseless witness or adversary in a hearing that they controlled, they were also shown to be cowards, sycophantic mediocrities and dissemblers. Every negative thing the public had believed about the political class turned out to be more than true, and many of these people, abandoned by the donors for whom they no longer had any value, wandered in the wilderness, often turning to alcohol and drugs.

And there were the corporate and financial criminals, the paymasters and string pullers. They made out much better upon release, although for many of them, being trapped in the middle of the former United States seemed like a continuation of their punishment. Most of them had been able to hide money, and, once out, typically went abroad. Some, however, began to exert control over the political and economic life of the Central Confederacy, often with great success.

After the American Civil War, there was a belief that the North had won and the South would now change. Instead, the opposite occurred. The North changed and the South became even more of what it had been. Over time in the 20th and 21st centuries, under the aegis of the Republican Party, the Southern ethos — racism, nativism, violence, ignorance, disdain for learning and oligarchy — became the national ethos. It ended up destroying the United States.

And now it would function without challenge over the vast center of the former United States, sinking into economic and social decay, violence and corruption. Meanwhile, the two coastal nations would struggle to create decent multi-ethnic and more equal societies, each with an ocean on one side and a pariah state on the other.

## HISTORY:

*A Final Note*

Like the election of 1860, that of 2016 was a seminal event in American history. In retrospect, so was the election of 2008: The ascent of a black man to the presidency had radicalized a significant portion of the white population and set the country on the path to disunion.

Then, in 2016, all the stars aligned to produce the greatest calamity in the nation's history. An iniquitous ego-maniac found the right formula to appeal to that radicalized white population. He had the financial support of a group of wealthy right-wing extremists. The Democrats nominated a weak candidate whose social distance from voters could not be papered over, although without the Russian connection, the felonious candidate would not have secured an Electoral College victory.

In a counter-factual addendum to their analysis, the historians posited an electoral win by the Democratic candidate, and far-right Republican dominance of the Congress. Despite her willingness to work with an extremist Congress, the House moved almost immediately to bring articles of impeachment against her. Impeached in the House, a long trial began in the Senate, with no chance of achieving the 2/3 majority needed.

Meanwhile, the country descended into chaos and violence, with all the threats made by Republican candidates during the campaign, about "Lock her up" and "Second Amendment solutions" coming home to roost. In a fundamental way, the outcome would have been similar for a polarized nation in which large numbers of people were happy to believe the steady stream of lies that they received from their preferred outlets.

Sometimes history catches up to you. The future always arrives. Americans, including many who should have known better, ignored the historian T.W. Maitland's warning, "We should always beware that what now lies in the past once lay in the future."

FRANK SCHNEIGER

# ABOUT
## THE AUTHOR

Frank Schneiger is a former government official and the founder and Chief Executive Officer of Frank Schneiger and Associates, a planning and organizational development firm. This is his second book. He lives in New York City.

FRANK SCHNEIGER

96510349R00133

Made in the USA
Columbia, SC
29 May 2018